IN SEARCH OF THE CITY
ON A HILL

IN SEARCH OF THE CITY ON A HILL

The making and unmaking of an American myth

RICHARD M. GAMBLE

continuum

Continuum International Publishing Group

The Tower Building   80 Maiden Lane
11 York Road   Suite 704
London   New York
SE1 7NX   NY 10038

www.continuumbooks.com

First published 2012

British Library Cataloguing-in-Publication Data
A catalogue record for this book is available from the British Library.

ISBN: HB: 978-1-4411-6232-8

Library of Congress Cataloging-in-Publication Data
A catalog record for this book is available from the Library of Congress.

Typeset by Fakenham Prepress Solutions, Fakenham, Norfolk NR21 8NN
Printed and bound in India

CONTENTS

ACKNOWLEDGEMENTS

This book would not have been possible without the help of foundations, librarians, archivists, friends, family members, colleagues, students, and editors. To all of them, I offer this simple note of thanks.

The H. B. Earhart Foundation once again provided generous financial support for a sabbatical and for travel and research in the United States and England. Hillsdale College's president and board of trustees granted me a year's leave for research and writing. Indispensable assistance with archival and other historical research came from the Massachusetts Historical Society in Boston, the New-York Historical Society in Manhattan, the Presbyterian Historical Society in Philadelphia, the library of Tyndale House in Cambridge, UK, and Hillsdale College's Mossey Library. The staff of these institutions patiently tracked down the most obscure references, documents, and resources. They gave of their time and talent, and opened their doors to me. A special word of thanks to the Massachusetts Historical Society and the New-York Historical Society for permission to quote from their collections and to the Alfred Music Company for permission to reproduce some of the lyrics to "Camelot." St. Edmund's College and Tyndale House gave me an academic home in Cambridge from which to explore John Winthrop's world.

Receptive audiences at the University of California, Berkeley, the Institute for the Study of Christianity and Culture, and Patrick Henry College provided the chance for me to air my ideas and gain helpful feedback on early versions of the chapter on Ronald Reagan. Their questions and comments reassured me that the reading public would indeed see why a wide-ranging conversation about the city on a hill needed to be launched.

Chad Van Dixhoorn shared his expertise in seventeenth-century English religious history and his personal collection of rare Puritan commentaries. As so often in the past, he and his wife and family blessed me with warm hospitality. My extended family also hosted me on various research trips, and my brother Ken read early drafts of several chapters.

Thanks are due also to a number of my students at Hillsdale College, especially the members of my seminar on the city on a hill who always surprised me with their fresh insights. They and others at Hillsdale taught me more than I realize. At the risk of leaving out someone, I would like to thank David Landow, Liz Essley, Jonathan Gregg, Joshua Herring, and Alex Meregaglia. They made connections I had missed and offered help with research, often on short notice. Thanks also to Harold Siegel, my colleague in the history department, for help with Latin translations.

For the third time, my former editor and current agent Jeremy Beer helped me shepherd a book from idea to finished manuscript. He took an early interest in the project, pushed me on to completion, and sharpened my thoughts and words. And thanks, finally, to Rhodri Mogford, my editor at Continuum, and the rest of the staff in London and New York for their enthusiasm and careful attention to every detail of this book.

Introduction:
The hidden city

You are the light of the world. A city set on a hill cannot be hidden.
MATTHEW 5.14

Shortly after 11:00 a.m. on 4 March 2009, British Prime Minister Gordon Brown addressed a joint session of the United States Congress. He devoted much of his speech to the enduring 'special relationship' between the US and Great Britain. But the event immediately on his mind was Barack Obama's landmark inauguration a few weeks earlier as America's 44th president. On that day, the Labour Party leader claimed, the 'American people wrote the latest chapter in the American story'. He spoke of 20 January as a day of renewed hope for the world when 'billions of people truly looked to Washington DC as a "shining city upon the hill", lighting up the whole of the world'.

By calling the nation's capital – and by extension, America – a 'city on a hill' and the 'light of the world', Brown recited one of the most familiar lines in the liturgy of the American civil religion. The only surprise was that it was a British prime minister leading in this national ritual. The cadences of Brown's affirmation of faith did not flow as smoothly and naturally for him as they would have for an American speaker, but the invocation of American exceptionalism was unmistakable nevertheless. Early in his presidency, Obama seemed deliberately to avoid the language of exceptionalism conjured up by the 'city on a hill', but Brown's use of this sacred rhetoric suggested that even in the era of 'Hope and Change' these words still captured the essence of America in the eyes of at least the Anglo world. Indeed, Australian prime minister Julia Gillard struck the same note in her similarly effusive speech before Congress in March 2011. She traced her own infatuation with the city on a hill back to the thrill of the lunar landing in 1969. 'The eyes of the world are still upon you,' she reassured her Capitol Hill audience. 'Your city on a hill cannot be hidden. Your brave and free people have made you the masters of recovery and reinvention.'

Few media outlets in the States or abroad seemed to notice Brown's use of 'city on a hill', and if they did they did not speculate about his intentions. By calling America a *shining* city, the prime minister obviously meant to link Barack Obama to Ronald Reagan's trademark reworking of the phrase and to his optimistic vision for America, the same optimism the Labour leader said he admired in John F. Kennedy and Franklin Roosevelt. 'America', he had learned growing up in the 1960s, 'is not just the indispensible nation'. 'You are the *irrepressible* nation,' he emphasized. And to Brown that meant that the shining city challenged the entrenched status quo as the world's perpetually revolutionary metropolis. 'Throughout your history, Americans have led insurrections in the human imagination. You have summoned revolutionary times through your belief that there is no such thing as an impossible endeavor'.

A moment's reflection shows how quintessentially *American* Brown's performance was that day. His speech reads like a parody of American patriotic rhetoric. He told Congress and the American people what they already believed about themselves. An exuberant Congress responded with at least a dozen standing ovations. In their lifetimes, the members had grown accustomed to hearing their nation called the 'city on a hill', in the press, from the pulpit, and in their own campaign speeches. And thanks to blogs and other media outlets, the metaphor's meaning had never been more widely debated than it was following the 2008 election. For some, like Brown and the Democratic side of the aisle in Congress, Obama's election signalled the triumph of all the deferred promises of social justice imbedded in that phrase. His victory had closed a dark chapter in American racism and intolerance. For the new president's opponents, the shining city stood imperiled as never before in the nation's history. Obama's 'progressive' agenda threatened to extinguish the city's lights and end its long run as the world's model of economic prosperity and political liberty. The exceptional nation risked imitating the very Europe so many immigrants had fled. For an angry few, talk of the city on a hill had already slipped into the past tense. The city was not merely vulnerable. It lay in ruins. The task ahead, therefore, was to retake the city from its usurpers.

Behind this debate lies nearly 400 years of American history. In popular culture, the phrase 'city on a hill' has become so closely identified with Ronald Reagan and before him with John Winthrop that even Christians can forget that the words originated not with a founder of a colony but with the Founder of their faith. At the beginning of the twenty-first century, the United States has achieved near-monopoly control over the metaphor. Despite scattered references, nothing in the wider culture has the power to challenge the American nation's ownership of the metaphor.[1] Even the Church in America might not have that power. When a megachurch markets itself under the name 'City on a Hill', does it reclaim the metaphor for Christian use or only draw attention to how successfully America has appropriated it? People driving by might even think that the congregation's name is a clever reuse of an *American* metaphor.

The metaphor of the city on a hill comes from Jesus' Sermon on the Mount as recorded in the Gospel of Matthew. In quick succession, Jesus compared his disciples to salt, light, and a city, and then back to light again. He warned them – and clearly it is a warning – 'You are the salt of the earth, but if salt has lost its taste, how shall its saltiness be restored? It is no longer good for anything except to be thrown out and trampled under people's feet. You are the light of the world. A city set on a hill cannot be hidden. Nor do people light a lamp and put it under a basket, but on a stand, and it gives light to all the house. In the same way, let your light shine before men so that they may see your good works and give glory to your Father who is in heaven' (Matthew 5.13–16). Barely half of one verse, the city metaphor proportionately takes up little space in Jesus' sermon. In fact, its position between two references to light means the city can also reasonably be read as a subordinate part of that larger metaphor. Despite its small role in its original context, the 'city on a hill' has become the object of varied and conflicting interpretations that overshadow the rest of the passage.

Whether Jesus had in view only his chosen disciples, his followers in general, or the universal Church he promised to build, he clearly did not address the metaphors of salt, light, and city to the Roman Empire of his day. He could have done so. Others living during roughly the same era did just that. A century earlier, the Roman statesman Cicero combined two of these three images when he warned his fellow Senators at the time of Catiline's conspiracy that he 'seem[ed] to see this city, the light of the whole world and the fortress of all the nations, suddenly involved in one general conflagration'. Centuries earlier, the Athenian general and statesman Pericles had praised his city as a model to all the Greeks. Jesus, in contrast, gave these metaphors to his Church and not to an earthly kingdom. At some point in history – we will never know when – someone first applied the city metaphor to something or someone other than Jesus' disciples, to something or someone outside the boundaries of the Christian Church. That may not have happened for many centuries. It may not have happened first and only in America. But along the way it became commonplace to talk about America as the embodiment of Jesus' hilltop city.

It is not natural or inevitable that America should have been given this sacred identity. The path from first-century Palestine to twenty-first-century America is not an obvious one. Nor is the path from a sermon about life in the

Kingdom of God to blogs about national destiny. Along that path, individual Americans did something to Jesus' metaphor that changed it. Gradually or abruptly, intentionally or not, they helped remake the 'city on a hill' from 'a metaphor into a myth', to borrow a phrase from historian Michael McGiffert.[2] Even if we cannot pinpoint the exact moment of transformation, we will see in the following pages that at one time Americans chiefly used the 'city on a hill' to describe something transcendent and theological, and then at a later time chiefly to describe something earthly and political. The transition required nothing less than the unmaking of a biblical metaphor and the making of a national myth.

The metaphor of the city on a hill comes up most often these days when historians, journalists, and politicians try to trace the origin of some praiseworthy or blameworthy feature of modern America back to its alleged Puritan roots. They engage in what the Cambridge historian Herbert Butterfield called the 'quest for origins'.[3] They look for the source of what they love or hate about the United States and its domestic and foreign policies. They imagine how the Puritan exceptionalist narrative, supposedly embodied in the idea of the city on a hill, set the nation's trajectory toward civic and religious freedom, toward democracy, economic prosperity, and humanitarian benevolence or, conversely, toward genocide, capitalist exploitation, prudery, messianic delusions, and ruinous overseas adventures. The 'city on a hill' finds itself caught in the fierce crossfire of the battle to define the American identity.

But lost in this debate is another story every bit as important to understanding what the United States has become: the story not of how the metaphor helped make America what it is today but the story of how America helped make the metaphor what it never was. Judging by how many recent books promise to tell the story of how some invention or election or natural disaster 'changed America forever', the reading public seems to be addicted to narratives of transformation. Americans like to tell stories of redemption about the most trivial aspects of their individual lives and also about the grand narrative of their national experience. Scientific discoveries, charismatic leaders, and landmark events certainly have remade America. But Americans have also remade what they have touched, and from the Puritans to Sarah Palin, their handling of the 'city on a hill' has changed Jesus' metaphor beyond recognition.

Piecing this story together, I have been guided by a principle developed and refined over the past 50 years by the Hungarian-born historian John Lukacs. Beginning in the 1960s, he urged historians to pay attention more to what people do to ideas than what ideas do to people. Ideas are not autonomous actors in history. Telling their story is nothing like tracing the migratory patterns of birds and fish. Ideas are acted upon, used, and changed. Contrasting two great nineteenth-century novelists, Lukacs wrote that 'while Dostoevsky describes what ideas do to men, Flaubert describes what men do with ideas: and perhaps the latter may be more significant – certainly for the historian'.[4] That premise lies at the heart of this book. Put into practice, it has the potential to reorient how historians write intellectual history. In the case of America's identity as the city on a hill, the words stayed the same, but what the metaphor signified changed over time as human actors, some famous, some obscure, used it for new purposes far beyond the scope of Mat. 5.14. To borrow an ugly word a trendy interior designer might use, Americans 'repurposed' the city on a hill as they rearranged the furniture of the American identity.

Credit and blame for the metaphor of the city on a hill being 'repurposed' as an American myth usually goes to John Winthrop. Tracking the city on a hill through time requires first that we revisit the Puritan leader's famous address, A Model of Christian Charity, one of the most quoted and least read documents in American history. This discourse's place in American memory has a history of its own. It is far more than an artefact of a bygone era. It has become a standard text in high school and college history, literature, and political science courses. It now stands at the head of what has been called the 'American Scripture', along with the Declaration of Independence, the Constitution, Washington's Farewell, and Lincoln's Gettysburg Address. Its message is supposed to be one of the principal things that make Americans who they are as a people. Subscribing to it and obeying its injunctions makes them more truly, authentically American.

But Winthrop's discourse was elevated to that exalted status only recently. It did not always stand as the book of Genesis in America's political Bible. As late as 1968, it was still possible for historian Lee Tuveson to write his highly regarded *Redeemer Nation*, one of the seminal books on America's messianic identity, without once referring to the Model of Christian Charity or the city on a hill.[5] And yet just 20 years later, Columbia University professor Andrew Delbanco could note that Winthrop's discourse had been 'enshrined as a kind of Ur-text of American literature'.[6] What happened between the 1960s and the 1980s to make Winthrop's words retrospectively so important? In 1961, when John F. Kennedy's speechwriter Ted Sorensen launched Winthrop and his city into American presidential rhetoric, no one could have predicted that within just 30 years the metaphor would permeate the nation's national consciousness. By the time Ronald Reagan left the White House in 1989, it seemed difficult for any major politician to talk about America without mentioning the mythic city. *Not* mentioning the city on a hill became grounds for questioning a leader's patriotism.

The city on a hill's journey from biblical metaphor to nationalist myth, and the rise of the Model of Christian Charity to canonical status within the American Scripture, raises fundamental questions about the American civil religion. Why would political leaders, often with the public's hearty approval and cooperation, adopt biblical metaphors like 'city on a hill' or 'Good Samaritan' for the United States? What does the State gain by this manoeuvre? What does the Church lose? Most puzzling of all, why would American evangelicals applaud or even participate in these sorts of appropriations of Scripture?

American culture's use of biblical phrases can be so powerful that the original meaning is lost. If a local Barnes and Noble bookstore displayed a new title called *A House Divided*, would customers assume it explained the meaning and significance of the third chapter of the Gospel of Mark? Of course not. They would think immediately of the Civil War and the speeches of Abraham Lincoln. And they would be meant to do so. But the words originate from Jesus' reply to the Pharisees when they accused him of casting out demons by the power of Satan. 'If a kingdom is divided against itself', he told them, 'that kingdom cannot stand. And if a house is divided against itself, that house will not be able to stand'. Words that had endured for over 1,800 years as Jesus' own suddenly became Lincoln's words – and with such force and endurance that it is hard to imagine them ever being reclaimed by the Church. Lincoln's success as a rhetorician and his gift for memorable turns of phrase do not mean that he intended to empty these words of their original significance. But thanks to him, and historians and political theorists who write about the wartime president, the nation added another metaphor to its narrative while the church lost one.

At times, political rhetoric claims for the nation-state things that Christians are taught to regard as true only of the Church or of Christ himself. Two examples help make the case. If a president claimed that 'the gates of Hell shall not prevail against' American ideals, would Christians be offended? Well, Lincoln said that. If another president said, again regarding America's ideals, that 'the light shined in darkness and the darkness did not overcome it', would Christians be offended? Well, George W. Bush said that in 2002 on the first anniversary of the terrorist attacks of 9/11. Did Christians notice? Did anyone notice the president's quotation from the first chapter of the Gospel of John, a passage that describes the mission of the *Logos*, the incarnate Son of God?

My interest in how America became the city on a hill fits into a larger quest to understand the images Americans have used over the course of 400 years to explain who they are. I have explored these threads in the American narrative since I first began work more than 20 years ago on *The War for Righteousness*.[7] As my knowledge of American history has been enriched by the hard work of other historians and by many hours of conversations with my students, I have come to understand America's messianic consciousness as derived from something larger and older than the liberal Protestantism I wrote about in that book. The 'redeemer myth' comes from a deeply rooted evangelical impulse, whether theologically liberal or conservative, to remake America and the world in obedience to a divine mandate. An activist Christianity, though often secularized and politicized, has propelled America's reforming zeal at home and abroad to build an earthly city on a hill. The tempting image of the city has been and continues to be used by both the left and the right because it fits so effortlessly into America's identity as a propositional nation. Being a city on a hill means being committed to an idea and to the transformation of everything touched by that idea. The shining city in the American imagination can be used to justify any economic reform, tax scheme, energy initiative, immigration policy, or military venture no matter how 'liberal' or 'conservative'.

Before I undertook this current project, the metaphor of the city on a hill occupied only a minor cubbyhole in my thinking next to such phrases as 'God's New Israel', 'last best hope on earth', and 'manifest destiny'. It was one idea among many. I taught about it in my classes and planned to pursue it further in my research and writing. I had imagined myself discussing the origins of the city on a hill in one chapter of a comprehensive project showing how the American identity emerged as a composite image synthesized from classical antiquity, Christianity, the Enlightenment, Romantic nationalism, and Darwinian naturalism – a book I still hope to write someday. But as I looked at the accumulating notes, folders, articles, and books on my desk, I realized that a separate study devoted to the city on a hill alone was possible and that it offered the rare chance to extract one thread from a very complicated story to be used as a way to think through some important questions about the evolution of America's national identity; about the construction of the nation's civil religion; about the meaning of American exceptionalism; and about the serious implications for Church and State when Christianity loses ownership of one of its founding metaphors.

One of the books in the mounting clutter on my desk sparked my suspicion that the American people have not always thought of themselves as a city on a hill or, more precisely, have not always thought of themselves as that city in quite the way we have been taught to expect. Thanks to that old book, I caught a glimpse of the possibility that no straight line runs from John Winthrop to Ronald Reagan, nothing at all like the kind of simple story Reagan himself often told. The book was John Wingate Thornton's *The Pulpit of the American Revolution*, published in 1860 on the eve of the Civil War. In the introduction, Thornton offered an account of what to his mind was the long-standing pattern (and therefore the normative precedent) of close cooperation in America between religion and politics since the Puritans first fled from Archbishop Laud at the time of Charles I. The striking thing to me as I read his introduction was that amid his discussion of John Winthrop, the charter of the Massachusetts Bay Company, and the religious motives propelling the Puritans across the Atlantic, Thornton never once mentioned Winthrop's Model of Christian Charity, today the most-cited origin for the famous metaphor of the city. The flagship *Arbella*, the Model of Christian Charity, and the 'city upon a hill' had all become so routine for me in textbook accounts of America's early years that I found their absence surprising. That silence demanded an explanation. It was, with apologies to Sherlock Holmes, the dog that did not bark.

Every student of historical method knows that it is risky to follow this train of thought and pursue an absence of evidence as if it pointed to something. As the old saying has it, absence of evidence is not evidence of an absence – meaning, the historian had better back away from any argument constructed out of something *not* in the record of the past, on something *missing* from a place where the historian in his wisdom thinks it ought to have been. Just because a neighbour's cat has not left footprints or a trail of mischief on his way through my backyard does not mean he did not prowl through it on his night-time adventure. Just because a historical figure has left no evidence behind does not mean he did not say and do all sorts of things that never made their way into a surviving document for the historian to find someday.

But I do not think this good advice covers all the justifications there may be for the historian to take note of missing pieces from the past. Some things truly are conspicuous by their absence, no matter how clichéd that old saying is. Historically, a significant gap might be evidence of someone in the past not noticing something or choosing not to comment on something that we in our own time consider to be indispensable. And this 'absence' – or, rather, our *perception* of an absence in the record of the past – might tell us something about ourselves, about how our thinking or self-perception has changed, and about changing fashions in history. Maybe the *absence* of evidence in one place helps us to see the *presence* of evidence in another.

If this is too hypothetical, then perhaps a concrete example may clarify my approach to evidence. In 1891, Joseph Hopkins Twichell wrote a biography of John Winthrop in which he quoted several sentences from the Model of Christian Charity. In the course of trying to explain the Puritan mission, the author quoted the sentences leading right up to the words 'city upon a hill', skipped over them, and then resumed his quotation. That gap tells a small part of an important story. We will put Twichell in his context later in this book, but for now we simply have to note that his eye was not drawn to these words. He chose not to cite the metaphor of the city as the definitive, inescapable expression of the Puritan 'errand in the wilderness'. Can we imagine a twenty-first-century historian, political theorist, journalist, politician, or anyone else with a stake in getting the American identity 'right' omitting these words from Winthrop's discourse? How could anyone omit 'city on a hill' from what after all is supposed to be Winthrop's 'City on a Hill' speech? The point is clear:

today almost every American includes by second nature something easily left out of the story a century ago. Enough missing pieces like these tell a story of their own, a story about how the script of American history changes from generation to generation. In 2009 and 2011, Gordon Brown and Julia Gillard thought they were telling Congress and their CSPAN television audience an obvious story about America, but prior generations did not find the meaning of the 'city on a hill' so obvious.

From these first sparks of curiosity grew a whole set of questions guiding my search for how America became the city on a hill. Putting Thornton's and Twichell's books aside, I wondered if it might turn out that Americans in the nineteenth century rarely called themselves the city on a hill or used the phrase in a way unlike modern Americans' habit of speech. What if as late as the Civil War or even the Spanish-American War these now overly familiar words weren't yet part of the stock of the nation's national metaphors? And if it turned out that they weren't, then at what point and by what means did they become so prominent in America's self-understanding? What if this contribution to the American myth is of surprisingly recent origin? What if what we think has 'always' been true about America's identity goes back only 100 years or less and not in an unbroken line back to the Puritans? What would that unexpected truth tell us about the difference between self-image and history, between false memories and reality? What if America has been divided by a plurality of conflicting self-understandings since colonial times and just one of those understandings – or even just a later version of one of those understandings – became so loud and insistent that it managed to drown out all the others?

All these questions and more arise from any close scrutiny of the story of America as the 'city on a hill.' Some of the answers surprised me. Some forced me to change the direction of my analysis. Some of the evidence turned out to be inconvenient intrusions complicating an already messy story. Some of the answers may make some readers uncomfortable. But history does not owe Americans, or any other people, stories that make them feel good about themselves. By the end of this book, some readers may wonder where the value lies in peeking behind a metaphor like this at a time when the nation is being tested so severely at home and abroad. What good could it possibly do, especially to the rising generation, to undermine any part of the nation's civil religion? If Americans become too self-conscious about the metaphor, it might be feared, then they risk not being able to use it without cynicism or an ironic smirk. Metaphors like these might be one of the few things unifying 300 million people who are bound together by little else than vague aspirations. The unexamined, unselfconscious metaphor of the city might be part of the drapery that keeps America decently clothed as a nation. In that case, a more chastened use of the city on a hill would be called for rather than abandoning it entirely.

I have asked myself these questions at every step of my investigation. I do not plunge into the story of how America became the city on a hill lightly or recklessly. This is not an act of vandalism. As a historian, I believe it is possible to ask all these hard questions only once we have traveled back across time and struggled to piece together the story of the American identity. The questions themselves are the product of historical comparison and investigation. As an American, I fear that the metaphor of the city on a hill has become an impediment to wisdom. One of the most important things I have learned from this study is that a slogan like 'city on a hill' can become a substitute for national self-knowledge rather than a genuine expression of American principles. Americans can delude themselves into thinking that these metaphors capture their essence as a people when in fact they distract them from the truth. As a Christian, I believe that for the health of the Church it is necessary to unmake a national myth in order to reclaim it as a biblical metaphor.

If I have done my job, then by the end of this book readers will be able to see and hear new things in the world – things they have not noticed before. The metaphor of the city on a hill vanishes into America's political rhetoric the way a repeated pattern disappears into busy wallpaper. My goal is to help the phrase 'city on a hill' stand out once again from the background noise, to help the hidden city become visible once more. My greatest hope is that this heightened awareness will lead to a serious conversation among conservatives and liberals, Christians and non-Christians, about what it has meant in the past – and what it ought to mean now and in the future – for their nation to be a city on a hill.

1

A foreign country

The past is a foreign country: they do things differently there.
L. P. HARTLEY, *THE GO-BETWEEN*

Nearly 400 years separate modern America from Puritan New England, as much historical distance as separated the Puritans themselves from the signing of Magna Carta in 1215 – a vast expanse of time. In order to understand the Puritans, we have to imagine a time and place alien to the world Americans have made for themselves in the twenty-first century. The English colonists in North America knew nothing of cell phones, cable television, or the Internet; nothing of interstate highways, agribusiness, or mass democracy. They had never heard of the Declaration of Independence, the Constitution, or a nation called the United States of America. They certainly did not know that one day they would be claimed as the direct ancestors of the American experiment. When we encounter the Puritans we do so from a world these settlers could not have imagined ever existing, a world that might well have frightened them if they could have seen it. Indeed, it is worth asking if the Puritans would call their godly commonwealth a success if they caught a glimpse of modern America as their offspring. We often talk as though they would. But they would no doubt be shocked by national crime statistics, divorce rates, traffic jams, and urban blight, and even by some of the things Americans are proudest of – their religious pluralism and democratic values, their tolerance and diversity, their secular sophistication and cosmopolitanism. The Puritans largely failed to create the world they imagined.

The distance that makes the past a 'foreign country' may disturb those who think of history primarily in terms of how it can be used to justify the way we think and behave in the present, in terms of how, in this case, the Puritans made America what it is today. By emphasizing the strangeness of the past, moreover, we may seem to remove it so far from our own experience that it ceases to be of much use in the practical task of understanding America and its role in the modern world. But if we lose something in the process, we also gain a perspective indispensable to genuine historical understanding. We gain the ability – real though imperfect – to see the past with fresh eyes, to confront the past on its own terms and not as a story reduced and simplified into a rough draft of who we are today. Once we grasp just how much time and experience lies between the modern world and the Puritan past, we are then free to think about what the city on a hill likely meant in another time and place and to observe with keener insight what generations of Americans did to the metaphor. The value of such an undertaking may be obvious to professional historians, but it is not so obvious to other serious students of the past who have not had a chance to cultivate the same habits of mind.

In order to help readers encounter the city on a hill as if for the first time, the first two chapters of this book set out to free the Puritans, John Winthrop, and the Model of Christian Charity from nearly 400 years of accumulated clutter. That is no small task. But a fresh reading of the Model is the only way to recognize just how many layers of interpretation have been added to the Model and its metaphor over the years and what those layers have done to obscure not only historic Christian interpretations of Matthew 5.14, but also Winthrop's intentions in 1630, and, ultimately, the full significance of later re-readings of the metaphor that did so much to secularize and politicize the city on a hill. A fresh reading enables us see the difference between Jesus and Winthrop and with that in mind then the difference between Winthrop himself and later generations of preachers, statesmen, and foreign observers. To that end, the third chapter of this book follows the fate of the metaphor in the theology of Jonathan Edwards and in the thought of a handful of other notable figures. Many took part in 'Americanizing' the city on a hill. These voices, spanning from the Puritans to the 1830s, reveal the expected and unexpected ways in which Americans turned Jesus' metaphor into a national myth. Only in contrast to the historical background assembled in these first three chapters will the full magnitude of the legends and false memories of later centuries become obvious.

Rediscovering John Winthrop and the Puritans as a foreign country requires first that we reconsider the story we think we already know. Most of us carry around in our heads pictures of the past that we did not consciously put there. Even if we have never visited Paris or Versailles, for instance, we have a facsimile of the drama of the French Revolution in our minds. Pause for a moment to conjure up a mental picture of the Puritan voyage to the New World. No matter how fuzzy that picture is, something springs to mind the moment you hear the word 'Puritans'. Maybe you confuse them with the Pilgrims and think immediately of elementary school Thanksgiving pageants (I was a rather bored-looking Indian brave and have a newspaper clipping to prove it). What year did the Puritans arrive in Massachusetts Bay? Is John Winthrop part of the story? How many colonists came with him and on how many ships? Do you picture at most a few dozen passengers huddled on the decks of the *Arbella*? Or maybe it was the *Mayflower*. . . .

If you know something a bit more substantial about the Puritans, that knowledge likely came your way from a high school or college history course. Here is one summary paragraph from a widely used college textbook called *America: A Narrative History*:

> In 1630 the *Arbella*, with John Winthrop and the charter aboard, embarked with six other ships for Massachusetts. In "A Modell of Christian Charity," a

speech delivered on board, Winthrop told his fellow Puritans that "we must consider that we shall be a city upon a hill" – a shining example of what a truly godly community could be. By the end of 1630, seventeen ships bearing 1,000 more colonists had arrived in Massachusetts. As settlers – Puritan and non-Puritan – poured into the region, Boston became the chief city and capital.[1]

This account, though highly compressed, includes some well-documented details: the year of the venture, the name of the ship, John Winthrop's leadership, the size of the fleet that set out (seven ships in all) and the surprising number of settlers in the first year alone (more than a thousand). As will become evident later in our search, this paragraph is interesting, though not unique, for what it chooses to emphasize and what that narrow selection of details reveals about how historians have reduced the complex story of the Bay Colony into a formula better suited to the 'city on a hill' as national myth than as Puritan metaphor.

Uncovering the metaphor's meaning and purpose in something even close to its original form requires that we momentarily suspend our knowledge of what happened after 1630. The use to which later generations put the metaphor is a different historical problem from what it meant in its own context. Understanding John Winthrop, his Model of Christian Charity, and his vision of a city on a hill demands that we try to see what the world looked like to an English Puritan in the spring of 1630 when the voyage to North America was a current event, when their colony was something expected and not yet experienced. From that vantage point, no comparison was possible between the Puritans and twenty-first century America. The Puritans thought largely in terms of what had happened in their own English past and what was happening at that moment in their native land and in Europe and the world. Like any other people, they certainly imagined what the future might hold, but the future still belonged to the realm of anticipation and not to their current experience or to their stock of memory. They could not connect the dots from themselves to something called 'American history'. They lived and thought, worshiped and worked, with something else in mind.

By 1630, North America had been open to European colonization for nearly 140 years. An English subject alive in 1630 had never known a world without overseas expansion. The Spanish had founded St. Augustine in 1565 and Santa Fe in 1610. The French had founded the city of Quebec in 1608. By the time of the Puritan venture, the English had already established Jamestown (1607), Bermuda (1612), Plymouth (1620), Saint Christopher in the West Indies (1623), and Salem in New England (1626). Despite the impression made by countless textbooks over the centuries, Massachusetts Bay Colony was never the starting point for the story of British North America. Tracing the trajectory of American history from this single point of origin means that historians neglect, or deliberately write out of the story, every other area of English and European settlement. They downplay or ignore altogether the Middle Colonies, the South, and even other parts of New England that weren't distinctively Puritan. By entering back into the world of 1630, we see that the Massachusetts Bay Colony was one venture among many, and one not certain to succeed. The Puritans came as part of an expanding English empire, subjects of a monarch to whom they owed fidelity, members of the Church of England into which they had been born and baptized, many of them graduates of Cambridge University, proudly English in language and culture, and tied by kinship and memory to their homes in East Anglia. As flattering as they might have found the honour, they did not comprise the first sentence of the first chapter of a new book but merely the most recent installment of a serial adventure long underway. In hindsight, these colonists may well have stood at a turning point in history, a moment filled with potential for the future, but in their own time they were a link between the Old World and the New, and in many ways they tried to make their new land look and feel like the old land they had left behind. True, they were reformers, and they hoped in some important ways to remake their church and their commonwealth, but they brought much of their English world with them, religiously, politically, economically and socially.

If we were able to look around England in the late-sixteenth and early-seventeenth centuries, ignorant of what came next in the story, it would be hard for us to spot John Winthrop. He was not a celebrity. Any modern observer unaware of Winthrop's later contribution to the founding of the Massachusetts Bay Colony would have little reason to notice him coming and going in and around his family estate in the Stour Valley. He was born in Queen Elizabeth's reign in 1588 (the same year as Thomas Hobbes) and died in 1649. His life, therefore, spanned the turbulent years from the attempted invasion of the Spanish Armada, through the Civil Wars, to the beheading of King Charles I. His grandfather, Adam Winthrop, had purchased former abbey lands at the time of the dissolution of the monasteries under Henry VIII. In this way, the ambitious Winthrops became owners of a large estate at Groton, a short walk from the village of Boxford in rural Suffolk on the road from Cambridge to Ipswich. The manor house no longer stands, but the church of St. Bartholomew's in Groton has become something of a shrine to the memory of John Winthrop. Since the mid-nineteenth century, Winthrop's American descendents have helped maintain the old parish church and have memorialized their distinguished ancestor in stained-glass windows and bronze plaques.

Winthrop attended Trinity College, Cambridge, for a couple of years but never took a degree. He returned to the family estate, married at the age of 17 (the first of three marriages), reared his children, studied law, served as a local justice of the peace, and prepared to assume his responsibilities as lord of the manor. At some point he joined the Puritan cause, a loosely coordinated movement within the Church of England to rid it of the alleged vestiges of Roman Catholic theology, liturgy, and forms of governance. The Puritans longed to reclaim, in their words, the 'purity of the ordinances', meaning the worship of God that fully conformed not to the Book of Common Prayer or to the will of bishops but to the Bible alone. For the time being, they wished to work from within the Church of England, from the pulpits and pews of their parish churches, to cleanse it and align it with God's revealed will.

The English Puritans often turned for guidance in theology and practice to John Calvin's *Institutes of the Christian Religion*, available to them in its final Latin edition since 1559 and in English since 1561. Winthrop left his own Latin edition to Harvard College in his will. In the *Institutes*, the Puritans read (in Book IV) the French Reformer's discussion of the 'marks of the church' – those attributes that make a church a true church. 'Wherever we see the Word of God purely preached and heard, and the sacraments administered according to Christ's institution', Calvin assured his readers, 'there, it is not to be doubted, a church of God exists'. Thus, the Word and the sacraments of baptism and the Lord's Supper, faithfully preached and rightly administered, became the means by which God's authentic church could be recognized and preserved. When the Puritans defended the purity of God's ordinances, then, this is largely the formulation they had in mind, though at times they expanded the divine ordinances to include the kind of 'godly government' necessary to protect and nourish the true church. The two institutions of 'church and commonwealth' often appeared together in their letters, sermons, and treatises. They expected the godly magistrate to protect the church.

Achieving and maintaining the purity of the ordinances required that there also be what the Puritans called the *liberty* of the ordinances. Their frequent use of the word 'liberty' can lead to considerable confusion for those who think of liberty only in modern political terms. The Puritans sought not a generalized or abstract freedom for all to worship according to the light of their own interpretations of Scripture or their own consciences but rather the freedom to build biblical churches. Liberty meant the freedom to worship God in the way his Word dictated, not the modern freedom of religion in a pluralistic society promoted by a neutral, secular state. This difference points to one of the pitfalls in any attempt to see the Puritans as the founders of America's religious liberty and tolerance. Freedom of religion was something that circumstances later imposed upon the Puritans in the New World, a development they resisted violently at times, as the Quakers discovered. Their descendents may have credited them with laying the ground for this 'American' achievement, but the Puritans did not cross the Atlantic for the right of all men everywhere to worship how they chose. They came to worship God as His Word dictated and to enable their children and grandchildren to do the same.

The urgency of the Puritans' quest for purity can be heard in a sermon preached by the Reverend John Cotton at the port of Southampton just before the colonists left for New England.[2] Cotton, a classmate of Winthrop's at Trinity and one of the most trusted pastors in English Puritanism, would join the Massachusetts Bay Colony three years later. He had come around slowly to supporting the Puritan 'removal' to the New World, as he and others called it. The main topic of his sermon was a long and detailed justification for the colonists' departure from England to a 'land of promise'. But in the midst of giving his blessing to the venture, he spoke repeatedly of the purity and liberty of the ordinances. The greatest English Protestant heroes of an earlier generation, the group of pastors known as the Marian Exiles who had fled England during the reign of Henry VIII's Catholic daughter Mary, had sacrificed everything for the sake of the 'liberty of the ordinances', Cotton reminded his listeners. And they had gone into exile even before Queen Mary's persecution began in the hope of returning one day to rescue the true church. Even after coming to New England, Cotton still spoke of his own motivations for leaving England in terms of the ordinances. In a letter to a fellow pastor in 1634, he explained that he had come across the Atlantic to 'enjoy the liberty, not of some ordinances of God, but of all, and all in purity'.[3]

These repeatedly stated 'warrants' for leaving England help us to know the kind of world the Puritans envisioned their prospective colony to be. As

we will see in a later chapter, a few influential historians in the 1950s and
1960s emphasized the intense idealism or even utopianism of the Puritan
project, which they described variously as the Puritans' 'sense of destiny',
their intention to build 'a kingdom of God on earth', their 'divine mission',
their universal reform agenda, or even their 'millenarian impulse'. While
the historical record gives some justification for this way of interpreting the
Puritan errand, it points more often to a simpler motivation: the building of a
safe haven for God's people to live and worship according to the demands his
Word imposed upon them. In 1629, Winthrop himself said of New England
that God had 'prepared this place for a refuge' for those faithful souls whom
he intended 'to save in the general destruction' sure to come upon an apostate
and corrupt England.[4] A pure church could flourish in a new land and be
'an example of great use' to God's people. In that same year, he assured his
wife that God would 'provide a shelter and a hiding place for us and ours'.[5]
The American Puritans' reputation for revolutionary and utopian intensity,
deserved or not, obscures this more modest hope for asylum in a dangerous
world.

The call to seek that refuge in the New World divided the Puritan
community. It was not obvious to everyone that the flight to America was
good for the church or good for England. The debate continued up to the
moment of departure in 1630 and did not end even then. As the subtitle
of one publication in 1630 made clear, there were 'those that question the
lawfulness' of the New England project. While many later chroniclers found
it tempting to portray the Puritan 'exodus' as a divinely ordained point along
the trajectory of God's providence and therefore the obvious choice for a
persecuted minority to have made, at the time the decision proved agonizing
and controversial, and some even regretted it later. Indeed, historian Susan
Hardman Moore has estimated that perhaps one in four of the Puritan settlers
in the first few decades returned home to England. The figure for pastors was
higher and for Harvard graduates higher still.[6] The Puritans of 1630 had to

decide whether or not to leave England based on their understanding of God's will and providential care and what they hoped or feared the future would hold for themselves, their families, their communities, and their churches. They asked what would come of those who did not have the means to pay for the expensive journey and begin life over again someplace else. What of those tied to England by family obligations or by their livelihood? Was it right to abandon these duties and one's God-given vocation? Was it right for their pastors to leave their parishes? What would become of God's flock in England if the best and brightest of the university-trained clergy packed up and fled? Did not Scripture and the history of Christian martyrs teach that God's faithful should stand firm under persecution? What if God had called his ministers to endure tribulation to the point of death rather than 'remove' to a new place?

These questions are not hypothetical or the product of hindsight. In the late 1620s, the Puritan community in England was wrestling with exactly these problems. The answers weren't obvious. In August 1629, about seven months before the *Arbella* and her sister ships sailed from Southampton, the Suffolk antiquarian Robert Ryece (or Reyce) pleaded with Winthrop not to go: 'The church and commonwealth here at home hath more need of your best ability in these dangerous times than any remote plantation, [a task] which may be performed by persons of lesser worth and apprehension, which I could show if I had time to think upon diversities of reasons which might be produced'. Ryece urged his friend not to squander himself on 'vain hopes' but instead to follow his 'vocation here at home' and not in a 'world of dangers abroad'. Let younger men venture off to the New World, he advised his Suffolk neighbour. 'How hard will it be for one brought up among books and learned men to live in a barbarous place where [there] is no learning and less civility'.[7]

Winthrop, though indeed a cultivated gentleman 'brought up among books', joined the Massachusetts Bay Company despite Ryece's remonstrance. In March of 1629, the Company secured a royal charter for their proposed colony in New England. King Charles suspended Parliament that same month, and the established church made life increasingly difficult and dangerous for Puritan agitators. In August, Winthrop and several other leaders of the Company entered into a formal agreement to embark for New England the following spring. The venture was carefully planned, its scale ambitious. Eleven ships were set to depart from Southampton, the same port the Pilgrims had sailed from on the *Mayflower* ten years earlier. Foul weather of the kind notorious in the English Channel forced the ships to separate. Four sheltered in the Port of Cowes on the Isle of Wight in the Channel.

Among them was the flagship *Arbella*, named in honour of the Lady Arbella Johnson, wife of Isaac Johnson, a prominent member of the Massachusetts Company who had urged Winthrop to join the effort. The *Arbella* was a 350-ton vessel (about twice the size of the *Mayflower*), with a crew of 52 and armed with 28 guns. The ship finally left the Isle of Wight on April 7, and the passengers caught their last sight of the English coast three days later. The first ships arrived in the New World in June, and by the end of 1630, 17 ships in all had carried about 1,100 settlers to the Puritan colonies in New England.

The Atlantic crossing took about ten weeks. In that time, the passengers endured seasickness, boredom, and the threat of Spanish privateers. The Reverend George Phillips, a pastor from Boxted in Essex who emigrated with his wife and children, preached on board the *Arbella* on the Sundays he happened to avoid seasickness and also handled catechism classes during the week. These details come from the journal Winthrop kept almost daily from the time the *Arbella* sat in port in the English Channel until his death in 1649.[8] The governor seemed fascinated by every detail of navigation and life at sea but rarely bothered to note how he occupied himself on the long voyage. That peculiar silence leads us to one of the many odd historical circumstances surrounding the Model of Christian Charity.

Imagine for a moment 200 years from now, a historian studying the Gettysburg Address realizes that only one manuscript copy of President Lincoln's speech exists. A renowned historical society in a major American city owns the only surviving nineteenth-century copy. That copy, though very old, turns out not to be in Lincoln's handwriting. In fact, a note on the cover of the booklet containing the manuscript is in yet another handwriting and provides the only explicit connection between the speech and Lincoln's name, the occasion for its delivery, and the year it was written. Further investigation reveals that Lincoln's diaries never mention the speech but do comment on the dedication of the national cemetery at Gettysburg. None of his contemporaries, moreover, ever referred in writing to what came to be known as the 'Gettysburg Address', not even those in the audience at the battlefield in November 1863. Perhaps most remarkably of all, it turns out that the first time the so-called 'Gettysburg Address' appeared in print and then began to appear in histories of the Civil War was the year 2071, more than two centuries after the speech was supposedly delivered. Between 1863 and 2071, no politician or Fourth of July orator or historian linked the phrase 'new birth of freedom' to the Civil War, quoted Lincoln as believing America was 'dedicated to a proposition', or included the Address among the nation's defining documents.

This scenario is, of course, the stuff of fiction, not history. No historian will encounter anything so puzzling in the twenty-first century. Lincoln's landmark speech and the events surrounding it are too well documented. But the same cannot be said of John Winthrop's Model of Christian Charity. The only surviving manuscript copy of the discourse sits in the archives of the New-York Historical Society. It runs to just over 6,000 words and fills 39 pages of a plain booklet about five inches wide by seven inches tall. Despite its fame, it is not on display in a marble shrine like the Declaration of Independence or the Constitution at the National Archives in Washington, D.C. Rather, the carefully conserved treatise is stored away in a small box, occasionally displayed as part of special exhibits, and generally available to researchers only in a digitized image or photocopy.

Even a cursory comparison of the Model with originals of Winthrop's letters or his journal shows it was not written in his distinctive, nearly indecipherable hand. The document's cover – which supplies the only indication we have of its title, author, and date – is in yet another handwriting. The cover also has variants of some spellings from the body of the document and a few words appear to have been added at some point by a third hand. As mentioned, Winthrop never recorded anything about the Model in his journal. He noted winds and currents, rough weather and seasickness, sightings of suspected Spanish 'Dunkirks' on the horizon, and occasional sermons by the Reverend Phillips. But he provided few glimpses into how he occupied his hours at sea: none of the books he read, no summaries of sermons he heard, no theological debates, and no mention at all of working on, let alone delivering, a speech about Christian Charity. Farther along in his journal he included some of his speeches before the General Court of Massachusetts. One or two of these, such as the so-called 'Little Speech' on liberty, became well known to generations of New England schoolchildren. But not the Model.

Until recently, the only historical record known to allude to the Model at all was a letter from the Reverend Henry Jessey (or Jacie) to Winthrop's eldest son. The Suffolk pastor wrote to John Winthrop, Jr., sometime in late 1634 or early 1635 asking him to 'procure' for him, along with other items, 'the Model of Charity'.[9] It is impossible to believe that this request referred to anything other than the now-famous document. If the young Winthrop ever sent such a copy, it has not turned up. Stronger evidence for Winthrop's authorship surfaced in the 1990s when editors of the modern scholarly edition of Winthrop's journal found jotted inside the cover of the first volume, in Winthrop's own handwriting, a list of some of the verses and characters from the Old and New Testament he used in drafting the Model. It is easy to picture Winthrop consulting his Bible and collecting his thoughts on Christian love as he prepared to write. It is easy to imagine that he did so just before he began keeping his diary on Easter Monday in 1630 as the *Arbella* and her sister ships waited in port for the weather to clear. Perhaps the passengers had already grown tired and restless and Winthrop began to think about what would be

necessary to hold these people together as a community under trying circumstances. But all this is speculation. We simply do not know anything about
how Winthrop came to write his discourse.

There is no reason to doubt that Winthrop wrote the Model, but there may
be reason to doubt that he delivered it to a shipboard audience despite how
engrained this 'fact' has become. The dramatic image of Winthrop exhorting
his brave band on the deck of the *Arbella* has become a stock part of the story.
But it is pure invention – an appealing invention and harmless enough, but
an invention nevertheless. Even the document's cover page claims only that it
was 'written' aboard the *Arbella* during the voyage, not that it was delivered:

A

Modell of Christian Charity.

Written

On Boarde the Arrabella.

On the Attlantic Ocean.

By the Honorable John Winthrop Esquire.

In His passage, (with the great

Company of Religious people of which Christian Tribes he was the

Brave leader & famous Governor) from the Island of Great Brittaine,

to New-England in the North America.

Anno 1630.[10]

One scholar has speculated that Winthrop delivered the discourse in
Southampton, perhaps on the same occasion that John Cotton gave his
blessing to the venture.[11] Indeed, Cotton's sermon and Winthrop's treatise
strike many of the same notes, including mention of a promised land, a
'special commission', and the need to animate the work with the 'amity and
unity of brethren' and a 'public spirit'. More than one historian has found this
theory convincing; several have repeated it as established fact. The truth is
we simply do not know where Winthrop delivered it or that he delivered it at

all. No passenger ever recorded in a diary or letter that he heard the Model of Christian Charity in England, at sea, or anywhere else.

The inconsistent wording of the discourse itself leaves us disoriented if we rely on internal evidence to figure out when Winthrop wrote it. In the first half, the governor recalled how the Puritans' ancestors had suffered 'times of persecution here in England'. That word 'here' would logically seem to point to only one possibility: Winthrop and his audience were standing in England at that moment. That would seem to make Southampton a real possibility. The sentence makes no sense in any other setting than England. But several paragraphs later, Winthrop warned the colonists not to be satisfied with the ordinary means they relied on 'when we lived in England', adding that extraordinary means would be necessary 'where we go'. Now the past tense of 'lived' seems inescapably to point to Winthrop and his fellow colonists no longer being in England. Three paragraphs later, near the end of the discourse, Winthrop used the if/then language of biblical covenants to say 'if the Lord shall . . . be pleased to bring us in peace to the place we desire, then hath he ratified this covenant and sealed our commission'. We will consider in the next chapter why this covenantal framework was so important, but for now it seems clear from the wording of these three quotations, taken in the order they appear in the discourse, that Winthrop's orientation or perspective changed from the beginning of the document to the end. He started out 'here in England', but then England slipped into the past as he pictured the shores of North America ahead of the colonists. In fact, the discourse's last line refers to 'this vast sea', placing him and his shipmates on the Atlantic Ocean.

This textual evidence leads to the unspectacular conclusion that the cover page had it right all along. Or almost right. What are we to make of that mysterious shift in language? Winthrop started out 'here in England' as he wrote and ended up expectantly on the ocean. One simple explanation seems to account for the entire document and how its language changes. What if Winthrop, stuck for weeks in his cabin, with perhaps his Bible, commentaries on Scripture, and Calvin's *Institutes* handy, mapped out his thoughts on what it would take to bind his community members together and to help ensure that they would fulfill God's awesome commission? He may have jotted down some verses and exemplary figures from the Bible while at port in the English Channel, begun writing while 'here in England', and then finished his draft at sea. This seems to be the most straightforward and satisfactory explanation for when Winthrop wrote the Model of Christian Charity. He wrote it throughout the voyage.

To prepare his discourse, Winthrop relied on a fairly narrow range of sources. He drew some inspiration from John Foxe's *Acts and Monuments*, commonly known as *The Book of Martyrs* and a bestseller that went through multiple editions. We also know from the list of books in his bequest to Harvard College that at some point in his life he also owned a Latin commentary on the Gospel of Matthew and a Latin edition of Calvin's *Institutes*. But in paragraph after paragraph of the discourse the Bible stands out as Winthrop's key inspiration. Most often, the verses from the Old and New Testaments match, or nearly match, either the 1560 Geneva Bible or the 1602 Geneva New Testament, the English Bible widely used by the Puritans in preference to the 1611 Authorized Version approved by King James I – no friend to the Puritans and their reform agenda. As its name suggests, the Geneva translation was produced in the Swiss canton where John Calvin ministered, wrote, and taught for most of his career. The innovative Geneva Bible included the apparatus of a modern study Bible: cross references, extensive marginal notes, and introductions to each book. The annotations bore the clear imprint of Calvin's theology. The Geneva Bible also happened to be the first English Bible to divide chapters into verses, and Winthrop adopted this practice when he cited Scripture in his discourse, although he or his transcriber made a few errors along the way, making it difficult to track down all his references. Judging from slight but repeated changes to the wording and spelling of the Geneva Bible, it appears that Winthrop may have quoted from memory many of the Old and the New Testament passages he used. In other places he freely paraphrased Scripture and did not bother to give a citation.

The way in which the Bible permeates the Model of Christian Charity makes it easy to think that Winthrop intended it to be a sermon. Since at least the 1930s, historians have commonly referred to the Model as a sermon or, more precisely, as a 'lay sermon', reflecting their awareness that Winthrop was a lawyer and landholder, not an ordained minister. In its structure, the *Arbella* discourse certainly does resemble the classic Puritan sermon format as developed by the Cambridge minister William Perkins in his influential book, *The Art of Prophesying*. The Puritan sermon style typically emphasized both 'doctrine and life' and moved from exposition of doctrine to what preachers in that day called 'use', a general form of application that Winthrop and his fellow colonists would have heard countless times in England. The Model of Christian Charity follows that same pattern.

But Winthrop himself consistently called the Model a 'discourse' (as I have tried to do in these pages) and not a sermon. In Winthrop's day, according to the *Oxford English Dictionary* (OED), the word 'discourse' could mean 'reasoning' or simply 'conversation'. Either of these meanings would have suited Winthrop's intention. He certainly reasoned with his audience and tried to engage them in an internal dialogue about Christian love. But the OED further shows that in the 1600s 'discourse' could also mean what we generally mean by it today: 'a spoken or written treatment of a subject'. Calling the Model a discourse helps us to read it in a fresh way, free of all sorts of assumptions that the sermon as a genre imposes on the text.

If the word 'discourse' raises few problems, the word 'model' causes more than a little trouble. It appears on the first page of the actual text, so in this case we have a bit more to go on than what the cover page provides. At the top of the page appear the following words broken into two lines (keeping the original spelling and capitalization): 'Christian Charitie: A Modell hereof'. The old-fashioned word 'charity' need not concern us because Winthrop never used it in the discourse, preferring instead the word 'love' as found in the Geneva translation of the Bible. Whoever wrote the cover page rearranged these words into the familiar title we use today: 'A Modell of Christian Charity'. It seems possible that Winthrop's intended name for the discourse could have been 'Christian Charity' with the words 'A Modell hereof' added as a subtitle, a section heading, or even as a modest disclaimer for reasons we will look at in a moment. The directness of the title 'Christian Charity' certainly fits the content of the discourse. But we ought not to stake too much on this inter-pretation since already by 1634 or 1635, as we saw earlier, the Reverend Jessey was referring to the discourse as the 'Model of Charity'. Winthrop himself, moreover, used the word 'model' only once in the entire body of the work and not in the context of Christian love. At the very least, we ought to keep reminding ourselves that the title of his discourse is not 'A Model of American Political Theory' or 'A Model of American Economic Institutions' or 'A Model of American Foreign Policy'. His thoughts lay in a different direction entirely – the high calling of Christian love.

When we encounter the word 'model' today, we might hear it used in the sense of a scale model, as in an architectural model for a proposed building or a child's model airplane kit. In this context, 'model' has nothing to do with an ideal. Rather, it is a smaller (usually a much smaller) representation of the real thing. Alternatively, we might hear it used to describe something or someone exemplary, as in the character from Gilbert and Sullivan's operetta, *The Pirates of Penzance*, who 'in matters vegetable, animal, and mineral' was 'the very model of a modern major general'. But what did Winthrop have in mind when he envisioned a 'model' of Christian love? *Who* or *what* was the model? And *for whom* and *of what*? Was New England itself to be a model to others (perhaps to other plantations in the New World or other Reformed communities in the Old World)? And if this was the case, of what were these high-minded colonists to be an example? Of godliness? Brotherly unity? Democracy? Liberty? Primitive communism? Dynamic entrepreneurship?

Free-market libertarianism? All of these mismatched possibilities have been claimed on behalf of the Model of Christian Charity.

The biggest obstacle to understanding the Puritans presented by these questions may be that they get things backwards. Winthrop may have focused primarily not on the Puritans as the model in his title but on something else as the model *for* the Puritans themselves to follow, a standard of conduct they had to imitate in order for their mission to succeed. If that was so, then the right question becomes what was the model *for* the Puritans. Indeed, as the discourse makes plain, Winthrop held up a model – a model of Christian love – to his community for them to pattern their lives after, the way children trace around a stencil or template to copy a design. This way of reading the title takes us in the right direction and helps prepare us to understand Winthrop's main concern and why he devoted so much of his discourse to something other than the 'city upon a hill'. Winthrop clearly did envision his Puritan community serving as an example to a watching world. Near the document's end, he did indeed write that he hoped other colonies would one day long to emulate New England in its faithfulness to God, and he did indeed warn them that the eyes of the world would be upon them. But none of these true things about the discourse seems to be the reason Winthrop, or someone else, gave it the name 'Model'.

To help narrow down the range of what Winthrop likely meant by the word 'model', recall his own context in Elizabethan and early Stuart England. Words change meaning over time, sometimes quickly, sometimes slowly. As they change, they retain some of their old meanings. And words rarely mean only one thing at any given time. The word 'model' has lost much of its earlier richness. Before we get too carried away, the OED and common usage in Winthrop's own day show us that a model could simply be an accurate representation of another (as in a scale model) or as an ideal standard to be imitated. These meanings go back at least to Winthrop's youth. We find them in Shakespeare's plays. In the Christian context in which Winthrop lived and thought, he would have encountered both meanings. An individual believer would be expected to be a 'model' of Christ (that is, to bear the likeness or imprint of Christ as closely as possible) but at the same time Christ would also be the believer's 'model' (that is, the perfect standard or exemplar for him to imitate). There is nothing too surprising here. Indeed, later Protestants and Catholics would continue for centuries to eulogize an exemplary man or woman as 'a model of Christian charity'.

But the history of the word 'model' offers a few other intriguing possibilities. In his discourse, Winthrop referred to Adam in his unfallen state as 'a perfect model of mankind in all their generations'. Here he used 'model' to mean a representative type— specifically, the first man who embodied and stood for the whole human race. The OED shows that 'model' could also mean an epitome (that is, an encapsulated summary or abstract) of a larger finished literary work. Twice in his three-volume journal Winthrop used 'model' in this now outdated sense: first in reference to John Cotton and Nathaniel Ward each providing the General Court with a 'model' of law to assist them in drafting a judicial code for the colony; and secondly in reference to his own 'treatise about arbitrary government' of 1645 which, he says, 'he first tendered to the deputies in a model' and later 'drew it up more at large'.[12] In both cases, 'model' meant a concise version of a longer work.

Now Winthrop was free to use the word 'model' in the way that best suited his purpose in a particular context. But given these examples from his own pen, and given the fact that he used the word 'model' only once in the body of the discourse, it is possible that he classified his work as a 'model' in order to signal that it was an incomplete draft that he intended to expand later into a full treatise on Christian love, much like his intentions for his later treatise on arbitrary government. In fact, there are places in the discourse that seem only outlined, just the thing we would expect to find in a rough draft. In a section on what binds Christians together as the Body of Christ, for instance, Winthrop set out to prove his point 'by precept and pattern' but never explained the precepts beyond citing two verses from the New Testament. His thoughts seem barely sketched out here, the verses serving as placeholders until he could return to this section. If this is true, then Winthrop never meant to deliver the discourse or to publish it in its surviving form. By the spring of 1630 it was still only a 'model'. Perhaps the cares of public office over the next two decades prevented him from producing a finished, polished work.

One more piece needs to be put in place before we look closely at the content of the Model of Christian Charity in the rest of this chapter and the next: Winthrop's audience. Even though he may not have delivered his Model to a literal audience, as a writer he still addressed himself to an audience in his mind. Writers reshape their ideas in a constant dialogue with imaginary readers. Rhetorically, Winthrop's ideas had an 'audience' whether he delivered the discourse or not. Unmistakably, he wrote as a Christian to other Christians. He did not write to a modern, diverse, secular polity made up of believers and unbelievers – a severe limitation for anyone trying to apply his principles beyond the homogeneous and insular Puritan community. Instead, he presupposed a Christian audience that knew something of the Christian natural law tradition, a great deal about the Old and New Testaments, and a bit of ancient and modern church history. This was an audience that would feel bound by these authorities. Though the discourse begins fairly abstractly, it was not a blueprint for how to organize civil society in general. Rather, it offered the pattern of Christian love and mercy that ought to govern one outpost of the Body of Christ at a particular moment in redemptive history. It addressed earnest believers intent on doing God's will in the world.

Winthrop did not begin his reflections on the well-ordered commonwealth with a story about Man in the state of nature, or an account of the origin of civil society, a history lesson, or even a passage of Scripture.[13] Instead, he began with a categorical declaration about the work of 'Almighty God' and His 'providence' over the affairs of all men, not just Christian communities. Man's condition, 'in all times', Winthrop wrote, is 'that some must be rich, some poor, some high and eminent in power and dignity, others mean and in subjection'. This opening statement amounted to anything but a philosophical or theological grounding for egalitarianism, liberal democracy or Christian socialism, or a prototype for much of anything else later authors hoped to find there. For Winthrop's generation, as for thousands of years before them, social hierarchy was one of the stubborn facts about Man and the world. These were God's prescriptions for a fallen world that otherwise, if left to itself, would rapidly and inexorably dissolve into anarchy.

In the following few passages of exposition, Winthrop offered three reasons for this divinely ordained state of affairs, and they all centered on God's character. These 'reasons' may not satisfy modern sensibilities, but we ought to take them seriously nonetheless as a window into the foreign country of the Puritan past. First, this social hierarchy manifests the glory of God's wisdom, power and greatness: His wisdom by means of earthly 'variety and difference'; His power by means of the 'ordering' or arranging of these difference; and His greatness by means of the delegation of his kingly authority to the rich and eminent whom He authorizes to act as the stewards of His blessings to men of all ranks. Second, this arrangement gives God the opportunity to show the work of the Holy Spirit toward both the ungodly and the godly. How? In restraining the wicked (whether rich or poor) from violently disordering the world by conspiring against each other; and in enabling the 'great ones' among Christians to serve others in love, mercy, gentleness, and temperance, and the 'poor and inferior' among Christians to practice the fruit of faith, patience, and obedience. Third and finally, God arranged the world in a hierarchy in order to bind man to man: 'That every man might have need of [each] other' and be 'knit together in the bond of brotherly affection'. Winthrop's concern at this early stage in his thought was to exhort the rich and powerful of this world (his own rank in God's hierarchy) to remember that they stood in their high position not because God had rewarded them for their own innate goodness and natural superiority, but rather because they served as instruments in the outworking of God's common grace and the activity of the Holy Spirit in the world.

Winthrop's vocabulary, style, and punctuation (or lack thereof) make these opening paragraphs extremely difficult to analyse. My own copy is marked up with lines, arrows, and marginal comments and diagrams that are supposed to help me follow the logic of his argument. Winthrop's one indispensable idea seems to be, not the charity or love mentioned in the title, but the imperative of mercy. The Christian commonwealth must be ruled by the law of mercy. Both the natural law and the law of grace teach Man the duties of mercy in his relations with others in society. The natural law (or what Winthrop also called the 'moral law') governed Man in his 'state of innocency' before the Fall. In that state he and his kind were bound together as creatures who shared the same 'flesh' and as image bearers of their Creator. Whether or not the natural law continued to operate after the Fall in Winthrop's estimation, as was commonly held in the Reformed natural law tradition but obscure here, the law of grace (or what Winthrop also called the 'law of the Gospel') now governed regenerate Man in his relationship to fellow Christians and even commanded him to love his enemy, something not known in nature. The Christian is bound to other believers as a brother in Christ. The law of mercy under the natural law taught Man to 'love his neighbor as himself' (apparently as an extension of self-love) and to follow the Golden Rule ('do unto others as you would have others do unto you'). The law of mercy under the gospel, however, went far beyond these standards and demanded self-sacrificial love within the Christian community. This was the law of mercy that Winthrop expounded upon, the high standard he held aloft as the model for his community, and the very heart of his discourse.

Winthrop clearly envisioned his own nascent Puritan community and the dangers ahead as he next considered the 'duty of mercy' that the 'law of the gospel' required of Christians, especially in 'times and occasions extraordinary'. Turning to the New Testament for precedent, he emphasized that 'there is a time' for believers to sell what they have and give to the poor, even give beyond their ability, a time of 'perils' and a time of 'special service for the Church' – and this moment was such a time. Gathering all the biblical evidence he could from the Old Testament, the gospel writers and the epistles, Winthrop urged his community to give liberally, to lend wisely to their brothers if they could but to do so even at the risk of losing their capital, and to forgive the debt when the borrower could not repay. This conduct had been true of the primitive church, continued to regulate life in the Body of Christ, and had to be true especially of saints bound together in a 'community of perils'.

To reinforce his point, Winthrop added examples of self-sacrifice from the early church, the returning Jewish exiles who laboured side by side under Nehemiah's direction to rebuild the walls of Jerusalem, and the heroes of the Protestant Reformation familiar to his audience from Foxe's *Book of Martyrs*. He held up the pattern of Jonathan and David, Christ, the Apostles and the saints through the ages. And he longed for his community to be motivated to acts of love and mercy not by rational arguments about the 'goodness or necessity of the work' but rather by making such acts a 'habit' of the soul and the 'affections of love in the heart' thenceforth 'native' to them.

By this point in the Model of Christian Charity, before any mention of the city on a hill, a key assumption of Winthrop's political theology becomes clear. The governor sought to apply the biblical standards for the kingdom of God as if they were the blueprint for the earthly community he intended to plant in New England. He drew extensively from the Old Testament, the teachings of Jesus and the Apostles, and church history to map out a holy community ruled by Christian love, mercy and brotherhood. If, as a lay leader well-versed in Scripture, Winthrop had limited himself to exhorting his brothers and sisters to exemplify these traits within the church, there would be little more to say about all the good advice he distilled from the Bible and

Christian experience. There would also be little to distinguish his discourse from countless other addresses the Puritans had heard many times before and would hear again in the future. But Winthrop addressed a Christian community granted the freedom and opportunity to conform not just the 'ordinances' but all of life to the will of God. He expected his community to be a self-contained, self-governing ecclesiastical and political entity capable of bringing everything into conformity with God's Word. Properly guided, one corner of the world could be made right enough for Christians to live in with a clear conscience. Whether such a community could also sustain its biblical identity as 'strangers and aliens', in the words of the New Testament, was another matter. Generations of New Englanders would wrestle with the early settlers' precedent of trying to harmonize Jesus' distinction between the 'things of God' and the 'things of Caesar'.[14] Winthrop's blending of the sacred and secular shaped the Bay Colony for generations to come. America's identity as a city on a hill could appear plausible and desirable only in a system of beliefs that accepted this standard of conduct for earthly polities.

2

The good land

. . . they should become spectacles to all the world:
for thus he saith, 'A City that is set upon a hill cannot be hid'.
WILLIAM PERKINS, *EXPOSITION UPON CHRIST'S SERMON IN THE MOUNT*

If John Winthrop ever did find occasion aboard the *Arbella* to deliver his discourse, it would have taken him about 30 minutes to read the text to his audience. For the first 20 minutes or so, his listeners would have heard the governor's exposition on what human reason and the Bible taught about mercy as the binding property of an enduring commonwealth that looked and acted as much like the church as possible. Only near the end as Winthrop moved from 'doctrine' to 'use' (granting the sermonic pattern) would his audience have heard anything about themselves as a 'city upon a hill' or an explicit connection between their own experience and the entry of the Israelites into the Promised Land. They would have waited that long before their leader applied all his synthesis of the Scripture's teaching on love to their own community-building in the New World. Only in the context of the Model as a whole can we judge whether Winthrop used the 'city upon a hill' as his discourse's rhetorical crescendo.

A student in a seminar I once conducted at a small college in Virginia told me that he read the assigned Model of Christian Charity impatiently, wondering when Winthrop would finally get to the words 'city upon a hill'.

Realizing the implication of what he was saying, he sheepishly admitted that he had always thought of the document as the 'city on a hill' speech. By simply reading it for himself as a whole, he now realized it was about so much more. He could no longer use those few words as the prism through which to interpret the entire discourse. Whether he knew it or not, this student was in good company. Some scholars stare at the 'city upon a hill' so long, so intently, so narrowly that they see almost anything in these four words and then read the rest of the discourse as mere prelude to the 'real' point. Hoping to arrive at a definitive understanding of the Puritan (and by extension the American) sense of mission, they ignore the rest of the discourse. This is one thing that can happen when a phrase becomes famous out of all proportion to its original context and place in history. Like those Magic Eye pictures in Sunday newspaper inserts in the 1990s, we can stare and stare at the 'city upon a hill' until a 3-D image of modern America pops out at us.

Apart from the added cover page, it would be impossible to guess from the first three-quarters of the Model of Christian Charity that John Winthrop was addressing English Puritans on their way to found a colony in North America. An astute reader who had never seen the document before would be able to discern a few things about it fairly quickly. It appears to have been a discourse written by a Christian for other Christians. Its intended audience seems to have been a close but limited community of believers who shared a common experience and outlook. An expert in orthography would note that the handwriting and paper place the document somewhere in the 1600s. Scattered references to Bishop John Hooper and the 'Cutler of Brussels' (both from Foxe's *Book of Martyrs*) along with frequent quotations and paraphrases from the Geneva Bible would indicate that the manuscript was written sometime after the Protestant Reformation had swept England.

Then, almost without warning, the modern reader meets the word 'application' and comes face to face for the first time with these people, their project and the haven they sought. Seeming to be aware of how long his exposition on mercy had taken, Winthrop declared his remaining task to be 'to make some application of this discourse by the present design which gave the occasion of writing of it'. Barely a word up to this point had said who these people were, where they were, what they were doing and what they envisioned for the future. But the governor now quickened the pace and, limiting himself to only four points of application, considered what he called the 'persons', the 'work', the 'end', and the 'means'.

Winthrop never addressed these people as 'Puritans' (a pejorative term not often used within the movement) and certainly not as 'Americans'. Instead, he called the colonists 'a company professing ourselves fellow members of Christ'. In that one body, even if they were separated from each other by many miles, their 'bond of love' would unite them. How much more, then, he seemed to imply, would they be knitted together living in one community. This identity, even if it fails to tell us anything close to the whole story, helps for the moment to strip away years of accumulated interpretations and labels. It enables us to see these remarkable people, not trapped as historical artefacts, not as raw material for academic speculation hundreds of years later, but as hopeful, fearful human beings poised at that hinge moment in the spring of 1630. Winthrop's 'we' and 'us' is not the United States of America, not Stuart England, not even, I would venture, the larger Puritan movement. Rather, these pronouns identified simply himself and his fellow passengers – a company of Christians on a special assignment from God.

But what sort of assignment? Winthrop used the word 'work' to define these people more specifically than a generality like 'fellow members of Christ' conveyed. Like so much of the Model, this section is difficult to interpret but helps us to recognize the first generation of Puritans in America as they, or at least as one of their leaders, presented themselves. The 'work' itself was controversial. Recall how the Puritans' proposed 'removal' had divided the movement in England. Before the journey, Winthrop had worked through several drafts of a list of reasons for going. Now on the voyage itself he was still sensitive to the question of how the Puritans who left home could justify their decision to 'seek out a place' in the New World. As an answer, he proposed that two blessings had made the truth of their calling evident to all: the clarity of a 'special overruling providence' and a 'more than ordinary' approval from Christ's churches. Note the appearance once again of the conviction that events were out of the ordinary – extraordinary times and now more than ordinary approval to meet the exigencies of the times. These were ways to read God's hand in history, to discern his providential leading.

But of course the work Winthrop had in view aimed at something far more specific than merely moving from one land to another. These were not intrepid tourists, curious explorers or ordinary colonists. These refugees intended to make a certain kind of place for themselves and their children. Only life lived under radically improved conditions in that new land would justify their venture. Therefore the colonists would bind themselves together 'under a due form of government both civil and ecclesiastical'. Nineteenth-century historians interested in emphasizing the political, institutional nature of what the Puritans were up to, typically quoted this succinct passage about church and state. What Winthrop meant by 'due form' leads into a historical labyrinth of interpretation beyond the scope of this book. Suffice it to say, that 'due form' should remind us of the Puritans' intense longing for 'godly rule' and for the liberty to observe God's ordinances in all their purity. Such fierce determination to live under the form of church and civil government that best protected and promoted the purity of God's ordinances drove the Puritans into the New World. That was their work.

Having named the 'persons' and the 'work', Winthrop next provided, in one long sentence, what we might call the colony's mission statement. The Puritans' goal, he wrote, was 'to improve our lives', not in some narrow, material sense, but in order to be at liberty 'to do more service to the Lord', to provide for 'the comfort and increase of the body of Christ whereof we are members', in the hope 'that our selves and posterity may be the better preserved from the common corruptions of this evil world' and that these settlers might be able 'to serve the Lord and work out our salvation under the power and purity of his holy ordinances'. This may not be the most concise mission statement ever drafted. But it does a good job nevertheless of capturing Winthrop's driving religious motivation, or, if we want to be more cautious, his way of clothing the Puritan project in distinctively Christian language. No doubt political, social and economic ambition attracted more than a few of the colonists to risk hardship in New England, but Winthrop situated their reasons for transplanting themselves within a powerfully religious framework.

Looking at Winthrop's list, we can see why anyone trying to find an embryonic mission statement for the United States in this document would have to use something other than the governor's own summation. For one thing, it is too narrowly and explicitly Christian. Ambitious Americans may specialize in 'improving' their lives, but their goal is far more material than that of the Puritans. Serve the Lord? Build up the Body of Christ? Escape worldliness and worship God rightly? These are not national goals, liberal or conservative, Democratic or Republican. This is not the stuff of empire. It turned out to be easy to secularize the metaphorical 'city upon a hill' out of its context, but these more complex and less adaptable aspirations proved more resistant to the agenda of any institution other than the church. They did not become part of the useable past the way the 'city upon a hill' did. It is also worth noting that these ends do not sound particularly utopian or universalist either. Historians have tried to figure out what Winthrop meant by the image of the 'city upon a hill'. They have discerned a millennial, utopian, revolutionary, national mission for America in those four words. But Winthrop offered his own account of the goal of the New England colony – less dramatic and yet brimming with the sort of details that keep history from being tidied up to suit present concerns.

With the community's identity, work and goal laid out before him, Winthrop finally took up the question of the means necessary for these people, engaged in this task, to achieve their calling. Once again, he called both the work and the end 'extraordinary'. Naturally, an extraordinary task could not rely on ordinary means. What the Puritans had relied on in England had been good, but it was not enough to meet the harsh demands of the enterprise before them. The love that most other Christians merely profess, these colonists had to put into practice, had to cultivate as a habit of the heart and as part of their character as a people. In fact, Winthrop claimed that God would hold them to a higher standard than Christians back home in England. Why? As strange as it sounds, Winthrop thought of his company of believers as more closely belonging to God, as more nearly His than those they left behind, united to Him in a 'more near bond of marriage'. He wrote that a 'jealous' God would require the same 'love and obedience' of them as He once did from ancient Israel. We will have the opportunity to look at the question of the Puritan settlers' consciousness as a New Israel when we reach Winthrop's remarkable reworking of the book of Deuteronomy at the end of this chapter. But even at this point, the notion of a special relationship enacted between God and these Puritan emigrants, an especially chosen people out of a Christian land that was slipping into apostasy, revealed an element of Winthrop's political theology. By his account, the election of these colonists out of England for this special task paralleled the way the ancient Israelites had been chosen out of all the nations of the earth. It is easy to see the Puritans' consciousness of themselves as a chosen people – as an almost 'super-elect' people – as fearfully arrogant. But that consciousness also placed on these men and women a heavy weight of responsibility. Their theology taught them that Christ fulfilled to perfection the covenant that ancient Israel failed to keep. But the special covenant that carried them to the New World – a covenant of works and not of grace – obligated them to perform their mission to the letter or incur God's wrath. Their eternal salvation did not depend on this national covenant but their earthly success certainly did.

Winthrop called this divine mandate a 'special commission' from God. A nascent American mission may not have been present among the Puritans, but these New World settlers certainly imported a powerful sense of *commission* with them. Winthrop left no doubt for his real or imagined audience that this was God's special calling for them, above and beyond the general commission given to the church. The picture that made sense of his words was Old Testament Israel. Despite his preoccupation with Christian love, expressed at times with eloquence and pathos, Winthrop at this point used fear of God's displeasure to stress the awesome solemnity of the colonists' duty: God would deal with their failure more severely because of who they were and the unique work to which they had been summoned. God expected to have this commission 'strictly observed' in 'every article'.

Winthrop's choice of precedent from the Bible is an unsettling one, to say the least. He took it from the account of King Saul and the Amalekites found in the Old Testament book of I Samuel. Through the prophet Samuel, God commanded Saul, in the language known to Winthrop from the Geneva Bible, to 'go and smite Amalek and destroy ye all that pertaineth unto them, and have no compassion on them, but slay both man and woman, both infant and suckling, both ox and sheep, both camel and ass' (1 Samuel 15.3). The Geneva Bible's marginal gloss on this passage adds, 'That this might be an example of God's vengeance against them that deal cruelly with his people'. Some historians might be tempted to see this violent episode as a foreshadowing of the colonists' 'genocide' against the native American tribes as their own Amalekites, but Winthrop's point here was something else entirely. Contrary to God's command, King Saul spared the life of the Amalekite king and the best of the sheep and oxen, feebly explaining to Samuel that the people intended to offer the animals as sacrifices to God – a 'fair pretense', Winthrop added. Because of this disobedience, Saul lost his throne. The prophet bluntly told the ruined man, 'the Lord hath cast away thee, that thou shalt not be King over Israel' (1 Samuel 15.26).

How many speechmakers in recent years, reaching for an inspiring phrase to sum up the American sense of national mission, have naively quoted from the Model of Christian Charity beginning from the words, 'Thus stands the cause between God and us', not for a moment realizing that the word 'thus' connected the Puritans directly back to Saul at the moment of his greatest test. *This* is how it stood in 1630 between God and the Puritan community, the same as it stood between God and Saul when the king of Israel faced *his* special commission . . . and failed. The kingdom that 'should have been his reward' was squandered through his disobedience. The stakes were high, the parallel ominous. If Winthrop did preach these words on board the *Arbella*, and if anyone who heard him accepted the parallel between themselves and Saul, then this was the oppressive weight of responsibility the Puritans carried with them into the New World. Their covenant teetered on the knife's edge of their own obedience.

While the idea of covenant figured prominently in the Puritans' interpretation of the Bible and in their Reformed theology in general (as shaped by John Calvin and others), in using 'covenant' here Winthrop meant not God's eternal covenant of salvation but the particular arrangements for this unique enterprise. God had blessed these Puritans with the opportunity to draft articles of association. They had decided upon the appropriate means to achieve the work of planting a colony in the New World and had prayed for God's 'favor and blessing'. This community-wide covenant followed the expected if/then structure of any covenant, a reciprocal arrangement with God on one side and the Puritans on the other, blessing for faithfulness, cursing for disobedience. *If* God brought the colonists to their intended destination, *then* that deliverance would show that he had 'ratified this covenant and sealed our commission'. *If*, however, the Puritans turned away from God and their calling and instead greedily pursued 'great things for ourselves and our posterity', *then* 'the Lord will surely break out in wrath against us, be revenged of such a perjured people, and make us know the price of the breach of such a covenant'. *If* they became base, carnal and worldly, and neglected their commission, *then* God would judge them severely. Their whole venture would shipwreck – an irresistible metaphor as the *Arbella* heaved up and down on the swells of the North Atlantic.

In considering this dire possibility of failure, Winthrop returned to where he began his discourse, to his meditation on the bonds of affection that would knit the Puritan commonwealth together for the sake of its special work in the world on behalf of the Church of Christ. Echoes of his prior exhortation to practice generous lending, giving, and forgiving reverberated now as he neared the end of his discourse. This section has been quoted often in the past 50 years, perhaps read most movingly by Justice Sandra Day O'Connor at Ronald Reagan's funeral at the National Cathedral in 2004, and yet it is worth reading again now that we have all that Winthrop wrote up to this point fresh in mind:

> Now the only way to avoid this shipwreck and to provide for our posterity is to follow the counsel of Micah: to do justly, to love mercy, to walk humbly with our God. For this end, we must be knit together in this work as one man. We must entertain each other in brotherly affection. We must be willing to abridge ourselves of our superfluities for the supply of others' necessities. We must uphold a familiar commerce together in all meekness, gentleness, patience, and liberality. We must delight in each other; make each other's condition our own; rejoice together, mourn together, labor and suffer together, always having before our eyes our commission and community in the work, our community as members of the same body. So shall we keep the unity of the Spirit in the bond of peace. The Lord will be our God and delight to dwell among us, as his own people, and will command a blessing upon us in all our ways so that we shall see much more of his wisdom, power, goodness, and truth than formerly we have been acquainted with.

This beautiful, rhythmic passage displays the intensity of Winthrop's longing. He repeated the Old Testament prophet Micah's instructions to ancient

Israel and the Apostle Paul's hope for the Ephesian Christians but narrowed them down to this particular community in this particular time and place. And the last sentence of this passage implies that God's promise to dwell among his people, broadly understood in Christian theology to have been fulfilled in Christ once and for all, had again become conditional under these special circumstances. Winthrop's long ethical to-do list meant that the New Englanders' status as God's chosen people depended on their perfect obedience rather than on Christ's finished work of redemption. Since the apostles, the church as a whole had stood in Christian theology as God's chosen people and holy nation, the fulfillment of the true Israel. The church was transcendent and universal, drawn from every nation and language, and not provincial. But Winthrop's depiction of God enacting a special covenant with the Puritans made it likely that these colonists would come to think of the covenant in terms of a literal people and a literal nation living in a literal place. Too easily, the chosen people and the Promised Land became earthly, temporal identities for an abiding city, the makings of a civil religion at odds with Christianity.

The larger context in which Winthrop placed the words 'city upon a hill' tends to disappear from popular ways of telling the story of early America. The section quoted in the previous chapter from *America: A Narrative History* offers but one example of how textbooks slip into the habit of reducing the Puritan project in North America to just one part of one sentence of one speech by one leader – and a 'speech' that perhaps nobody ever heard. Compounding the problem, countless well-meaning teachers, bloggers, editorial writers, and politicians take it for granted that the 'we' in the phrase 'we shall be as a city upon a hill' somehow mysteriously refers to the United States – an odd assumption even on the face of it. Americans hear their nation's identity as the 'city on a hill' vigorously debated, but how many commentators bother to consider whether Winthrop could have possibly been talking about

America at all? Arguments between Republicans and Democrats over the meaning of the 'city on a hill' sound like they come from the two extremes of a polarizing national debate, but both sides assume the same dubious thing about Winthrop: that somehow he spoke prophetically about the United States. No matter how much the two major political parties disagree on domestic and foreign policy, they both assume that America, from its earliest days, was destined to be a 'city on a hill'. What Dorothy Parker famously said about Katharine Hepburn's acting skills applies to the debate over the city on a hill: it 'runs the gamut of emotions from A to B'. It masquerades as an ideological debate from the extreme ends of the political spectrum when in fact it is a narrow debate between two secularized, politicized versions of the church. Missing in all this is even a hint of doubt that Americans should call their nation the city on a hill and seek John Winthrop's (and Jesus') blessing for doing so.

After all the work we have done to establish the context for the Model of Christian Charity and to map out its central argument, we have not yet come to the phrase 'city upon a hill' – the phrase that so many around the world today, including prime ministers, assume defines Winthrop's message, the Puritan colonists' self-understanding, and the meaning of America. The celebrated words follow immediately after the section from Micah on doing justice and loving mercy. From Winthrop's vision of God's wisdom, power, goodness and truth, he moved on to his only explicit reference to New England and its place in the world, assembling fragments from the Old and New Testaments as he did so:

We shall find that the God of Israel is among us when ten of us shall be able to resist a thousand of our enemies, when he shall make us a praise and a glory, that men shall say of succeeding plantations, "The Lord make it like that of New England." For we shall be as a city upon a hill. The eyes of all people are upon us, so that if we shall deal falsely with our God in this work we have undertaken and so cause him to withdraw his present help from us, we shall be made a story and a byword through the world.

Before we surgically remove the phrase 'city upon a hill' from Winthrop's discourse and examine it in detail, we ought to pause for a moment to remind ourselves of the risks involved in this delicate operation. The seemingly innocent question of why Winthrop envisioned America as the 'city upon a hill' might not turn out to be so innocent. The fact that we raise the question at all tells us more about modern America than it does about seventeenth-century Boston. It is *our* question. It is a question generated more by our own needs in our own time than by what was going on in England and its expanding North American empire 400 years ago. Despite what we tell aspiring elementary school teachers, there really is such a thing as a bad question. Some questions have no answers because of the way they are constructed. More precisely, some questions are impossible because they are based on a false assumption. If someone were to ask me how long it took me to paint the ceiling of the Sistine Chapel, I would have no answer. I would be tongue-tied not because I was being modest or prevaricating but because the question itself has no grounding in reality. It is built on a false premise. The problem lies not with me but with the question. The question assumes I painted those frescos in the Vatican, but I did not. Similarly, if a teacher asks students to write an essay on the question, 'What did John Winthrop mean by calling America the "city upon a hill"?' there is no right answer. The question assumes something to be true about the world that never happened. There are not right and wrong answers to the question. There is no answer at all.

Winthrop knew the metaphor of the city on a hill from Jesus' Sermon on the Mount. He quoted the Gospel of Matthew at least six times in the Model of Christian Charity, and five of these instances came from the Sermon on the Mount, including Matthew 5.14: 'Ye are the light of the world. A city that is set on an hill cannot be hid' (as translated by the Geneva Bible of 1560). So extensive was Winthrop's use of Matthew that he appears to have meditated carefully on the Sermon on the Mount before writing his discourse. And given the extensive guidance found there for how to live in God's kingdom, his doing so would make sense, especially for a man trying to apply Jesus' ethical imperatives to the Puritan commonwealth he was about to lead.

Getting from Jesus to Winthrop took centuries, of course. Behind Winthrop's use of this metaphor lay nearly 1,600 years of biblical interpretation. In general, the Church Fathers typically gave more attention to the metaphor of light in Matthew 5.14–15 than to the city, and this tendency remained true among the Reformers and beyond. The early Fathers understood the city's visibility as expressing the same meaning as Jesus' point in the following verse about a lamp's visibility on a stand and its power from that height to illuminate the whole house. When these theologians turned to the picture of the city itself, they interpreted it in a variety of ways but always within a fairly narrow range and always in reference to the church.

Hilary of Poitiers, the fourth-century bishop who defended the Nicene Creed against the Arian heresy, understood the city to be Christ himself, uniting all believers as citizens of that new community. 'Therefore he cannot be hidden', Hilary wrote of Christ. 'Situated on God's lofty height, he is held up to all in admiration of his good works as deserving of contemplation and understanding'. Expanding the metaphor a bit, the anonymous early author of a set of sermons on Matthew wrote that the city 'is the church, the holy people, of which the prophet says, "Glorious things of you are spoken, city of our King"' – a common connection between the city metaphor and the Zion mentioned in Psalm 87. John Chrysostom, the fourth-century Bishop of Constantinople, in his own homilies on Matthew, interpreted the city as representing Jesus' disciples. By calling them a city, Chrysostom wrote, Jesus warned his disciples to watch their doctrine and their life. His followers would be 'set before the eyes of all men', as if 'contending in the midst of the amphitheater of the world'. Miraculously, Jesus took a group of obscure men and made them 'conspicuous' through their good works. These and other early writers, continuing on down to Thomas Aquinas in the thirteenth century, agreed about the meaning of the city: it was Jesus' metaphor for his Church as his own Body, for its ongoing teaching ministry, and for the conspicuous doctrine and life of his disciples and the teachers of the Word who followed after them.[1]

Looking ahead another 300 years to the Protestant Reformation, no radical break appeared at that point with the traditional consensus on Matthew 5 but instead a surprising continuity persisted – surprising, that is, for anyone who expects the Reformers to have broken with the Catholic Church in every possible way. Martin Luther modeled his commentary on the Sermon on the Mount on Augustine's similar treatise. Joining the metaphors of light and city, as had been common since the early church, the German reformer drew attention to the 'ministry which [Jesus] entrusts to His dear apostles'. The apostles were called to enlighten the world and to preach 'publicly and fearlessly'. And what Jesus said to his own disciples in his own day applied as well to the clergy of Luther's day, he wrote.[2]

Likewise, Luther's younger contemporary, John Calvin, saw combined in the metaphors of salt, light and city the 'preaching of the Gospel' that in times past was committed first to the apostles. Following after them, 'the Church's pastors are today given it[;] it is to them that Christ gives this exceptional title'. 'This was the condition of their being put into that rank', the French Reformer wrote in his commentary on the synoptic gospels, '. . . to leave the rest behind and give light from a higher post'. Pastors therefore had 'to live in a godly and holy way' because 'the eyes of all are turned upon them as upon a beacon'.[3] This last phrase, so familiar from John Winthrop and so often assumed to refer to America's conspicuous place among the nations of the world, came not from Matthew's gospel at all but from Calvin who echoed Chrysostom's ancient warning that the disciples, and by extension all pastors, would be 'set before the eyes of all men'. Luther and Calvin simply carried forward the long tradition that exhorted ministers of the Word to watch their doctrine and their life.

Winthrop, or our accustomed way of reading Winthrop, has so profoundly coloured these words from the Sermon on the Mount that Americans can find it difficult to read them with the eyes the church has used throughout its history. Indeed, one point in particular about Jesus' words ought to be obvious. In contrast to modern Americans, it does not seem to have occurred to any Church Father or medieval theologian or Protestant Reformer to interpret the 'city upon a hill' as anything but the church and its pastoral ministry. Historian Darryl Hart, looking at how Luther and Calvin interpreted the city metaphor, draws attention to what these Reformers *did not say*. They did not summon the kingdoms of their day to embody the 'city upon a hill'. And they refrained from doing so even when it might have helped their reform efforts' prospects of earthly success to elevate magistrates and dukes and kings to such a high sacred calling. For Calvin as for Luther, Hart writes, 'these instructions from Christ have direct reference to ecclesiastical rather than political affairs'.[4]

We have good reason to suppose that Winthrop himself knew the accepted way of interpreting Matthew 5.14. Among the books he left to Harvard College in his will was *In Evangelistam Matthaeum Commentarii*, a Latin commentary on Matthew by the German theologian Wolfgang Musculus. Musculus may be little known today, but he served for a time as secretary to the reformer Martin Bucer, was a colleague of Calvin's in Strasbourg, and his interpretations of Scripture often appeared in Puritan works alongside quotations from Calvin, Bucer and Heinrich Bullinger. Perhaps Winthrop consulted Musculus as he prepared to write his Model. If so, then he encountered the following explanation of Jesus' metaphor of light, a reading fully in line with the historic church: 'We see that the ministers of Christ, ought to be in stead of [that is, they ought to represent] the light, lightening the darkness of this world, because of the doctrine of truth which they show to the whole world'. Musculus's mentor, Martin Bucer, similarly emphasized the pastor's need to set a proper example: 'the heavenly doctrine and the life of the teacher must be godly, holy, pure, perfect, and irreprehensible'. And their contemporary Bullinger reminded pastors that 'as a city built on a hill cannot be hidden, even so ye cannot be hidden, neither ought ye, but ye shall be made manifest unto the whole world, even as a city set upon a hill. Wherefore by all means endeavor yourselves [so] that men may see that in you which is godly and virtuous to imitate and follow'.[5]

Turning from these leading Reformed theologians of the sixteenth century, do we encounter the same apolitical tendency among the English Puritans of Winthrop's own generation? It might be possible, after all, that Winthrop learned a more political spin on the city metaphor from his contemporaries. The Puritan pastor and theologian William Perkins, who preached in Cambridge until his death in 1602, just before Winthrop matriculated at Trinity College, and whose books Winthrop read, wrote of Matthew 5.14 that Jesus addressed his disciples and by extension all ministers: 'By calling you are the light of the world, and your condition is such that all your sayings and doings are open to the eyes of men: therefore be ye careful that ye glorify God therein'. By depicting his disciples as the 'light of the world', a 'city set on a hill', and a 'candle on a candlestick', Perkins continued, Jesus did not mean to 'give them titles of praise, but to make them acquainted with their hard condition, in which they were like[ly] to be by reason of their great and weighty calling, wherein they should become spectacles to all the world'.[6]

These few examples among the dozens possible, show the consensus and clarity among the English Puritans and among the wider Reformed community in Europe regarding the 'city upon a hill'. In short, being such a city meant that Jesus' disciples and by extension ministers of the gospel would inevitably be 'spectacles to all the world', in Perkins' vivid phrase. Jesus' warning to his disciples was interpreted first and foremost as a warning to ministers to watch their doctrine and their life. Be careful what you teach and how you live because you will be observed, whether for good or evil, whether for blessing or reproach. Winthrop's contemporary, the Geneva-born reformer, pastor, and translator of the Bible into Italian, Giovanni Diodati, whose work was well-known in seventeenth-century England, also wrote of the city's exposure as a warning to pastors: 'the eminency of your office shall cause all the good and evil that is in you to be manifest to all men, either for example and edification in good things, or for scandal and destruction in evil'.[7] Of all the commentaries on the metaphor of the city, this one seems closest to Winthrop's own purposes. The city on a hill served primarily as a warning, perhaps not as fearsome as the allusion to King Saul and Amalek, but a warning nevertheless.

And yet there is an important and interesting difference between Winthrop and these theologians. The Puritan leader took the metaphor and applied it to an earthly enterprise. He was not the first to do so, as we will see in the next chapter. And he certainly never manipulated the metaphor into a glib affirmation of God's unconditional blessing. But it is his application of it to something other than pastors and their teaching ministry that has become a celebrated part of the American identity. No politicians and few historians quote anyone else. And as he adapted the metaphor, he moved away from the more restrained practice of the theologians he read. Unwittingly and unintentionally, he helped shape the way an entire nation would one day reinterpret these words: '*We* must consider that *we* shall be as a city upon a hill. The eyes of all people are upon *us*' (emphasis added). Not pastors, not their doctrine and life, but the whole Puritan community. There was some precedent in Calvin (and all the way back to bishop Hilary in the fourth century) for expanding the scope of the metaphor to embrace all those believers united in the Body of Christ. Nevertheless, Calvin began with teachers of the Word and ended with pastors. Almost without exception, when the commentators of the sixteenth and seventeenth centuries said 'you' must be exemplary in doctrine and life, they meant those ordained to the pastoral ministry and not the church in general, not specific congregations of gathered saints, not earthly commonwealths, and certainly not individual Christians resolving each morning to be a brighter light in the world, shining for Jesus as their own little city on a hill. The Reformers' and Puritan theologians' view was far more churchly than civic, far more institutional than individualist.

We forget that the phrase 'city upon a hill' comes from only one part of one verse in the New Testament and that it occupies a similarly modest place in the Model of Christian Charity. It was merely one among dozens and dozens of Scripture verses Winthrop collected to write his discourse. And some of these passages mattered far more than Matthew 5.14 for the direction of his ideas. At the close of the Model, he reworked an entire section from the Old Testament book of Deuteronomy. He adapted it from what is often called Moses' 'valedictory', his farewell address to the people he had led out of captivity in Egypt and through 40 years of wilderness wandering. Because of his earlier disobedience, Moses himself was not permitted by God to enter the Promised Land. But as he spoke to his people from the heights of Mount Nebo, he could see the land of milk and honey lying across the Jordan River.

Putting Deuteronomy 30 from the Geneva Bible of 1560 alongside Winthrop's skilful reworking of it in 1630 gets us as close as possible to the picture Winthrop had in his mind as he summed up his own advice to the Puritans. This passage makes it almost irresistible to see Winthrop in the role of Moses – or to assume that Winthrop must have seen himself in that exalted role, the leader of a new chosen people crossing into a new chosen land. But the changes Winthrop made to the biblical text may indicate that he deliberately held himself back from these parallels, or at least from the most obvious parallels. The historical significance may lie in the changes he made to Moses' words and not in what he kept the same. Nevertheless the parallels are close. Even the change of the first word in the quoted passage from 'behold' in the Geneva Bible to 'beloved' in Winthrop's version seems to have been a copyist's error.

GENEVA BIBLE (1560)

Beholde, I haue set before thee this day life & good, death and euil. In that I commande thee this day, to loue the Lord thy God, to walke in his wayes, & to kepe his commandements, & his ordinances, & his lawes that thou maiest liue and be multiplied, and that the Lord thy God may blesse thee in the land, whether thou goest to possesse it. But if thine heart turne away, so that thou wilt not obey, but shalt be seduced & worship other gods, and serue them, I pronounce vnto you this day that ye shall surely perish, ye shall not prolong your dayes in the land whether thou passest ouer Jorden to possesse it. I call heauen & earth to recorde this day against you, *that* I haue set before you life and death, blessing and cursing, therefore chose life, that *bothe* thou & thy sede may liue, By louing the Lorde thy God, by obeying his voyce, & by cleauing vnto him: for he is thy life, and the length of thy dayes:

JOHN WINTHROP (1630)

Beloued there is now sett before vs life, and good, deathe and euill in that wee are Commaunded this day to loue the Lord our God, and to loue one another to walke in his wayes and to keepe his Commaundements and his Ordinance, & his lawes, and the Articles of our Covenant with him that wee may liue and be multiplyed, and that the Lord our God may blesse vs in the land whether wee goe to possesse it: But if our heartes shall turne away soe that wee will not obey, but shall be seduced and worshipp other Gods our pleasures, and proffitts, and serue them; it is propounded vnto vs this day, wee shall surely perishe out of the good Land whether wee passe over this vast Sea to possesse it; Therefore lett vs choose life, that wee, and our Seede, may liue; by obeying his voyce, & cleauing to him, for hee is our life, & our prosperity.

Line by line, Winthrop changed the biblical text to reflect his own circumstances. The Moses of the Exodus did not get to accompany his people into the Promised Land, but Winthrop had every intention of leading and governing his people in New England. Therefore, he changed Moses' first-person active commands into third-person passive circumstances. Instead of the forceful directive, 'I set before thee this day life and good, death and evil', we find in Winthrop the inclusive words, 'there is now set before us life and good, death and evil'. Winthrop, unlike Moses, got to be part of the 'us' about to enter the land. If Winthrop had seen himself as a perfect match for Moses, then he would have been barred from the Promised Land. If anything, Winthrop got to play the role of both Moses and Joshua. He led his people out of Egypt and marched with them into Canaan. Other changes appear as well. Where Moses warned the Israelites against idolatry, Winthrop defined the 'other gods' they would fall prey to as 'our pleasures and profits', consistent with the fear he expressed earlier in the discourse that riches and worldly ease would 'seduce' them from their special commission and incur God's wrath. And where Moses mentioned the Jordan, Winthrop substituted 'this vast sea' – the Atlantic Ocean. The mental image he conjured up, therefore, was not of the Israelites escaping from Egypt across the Red Sea. That step, after all, would seem to guarantee 40 years of wandering ahead of them. Rather, Winthrop placed the Puritan community all the way at the other end of the Exodus story. They stood together at the verge of the Promised Land.

It has become commonplace among historians and journalists to refer to Winthrop as the American 'Moses', to the Puritan project as the 'Exodus', and to New England as 'Canaan' or the 'Promised Land'. Biblical parallels of all sorts suggested themselves easily enough to the Puritans and to their descendants in America. One thing to bear in mind is that the modern idea of a chosen nation was not invented in America. Several scholars have shown that sixteenth- and seventeenth-century England thought of itself, in the words of one pastor in 1586, as 'we little Israel of England'. Some have discerned traces of this consciousness in William Tyndale's translation of the Bible and in John Foxe's *Book of Martyrs*. And England's elect status during Oliver Cromwell's Commonwealth became the stock in trade of obsequious poets. Historian Nicholas Guyatt writes of the belief in a single providential mission that for a time united England with her North American colonies.[8] If the Puritans who came to America, then, thought of themselves as God's New Israel, there would have been plenty of precedent for doing so. They did not have to invent the idea; they merely had to import it.

Coming out of that environment, would Winthrop have been able to imagine his colony as anything other than a 'little Israel'? This is a difficult but important question. Was Winthrop himself merely a 'man of his time' destined to think of himself and his mission in a predetermined way? Was he doomed to draw straight lines from the Old Testament to himself? Could he have been equipped theologically to do otherwise? It turns out that active alternatives to a political theology of chosen lands and chosen peoples not only existed but existed even among supporters of the colonization effort. A decade after the planting of the colony, William Fiennes, Lord Saye and Sele, rebuked Winthrop sharply for the way he spoke of New England. Unfortunately, Winthrop's initial letter to Saye (20 March 1640) that provoked his angry reply has not survived. But in the course of defending himself, Saye repeated enough of Winthrop's charges to make it possible to reconstruct a few of the more salient points of controversy between them. The crisis that provoked Winthrop to write to Saye concerned the nobleman's decision to promote Puritan settlement in the West Indies as an alternative to the cold and barren land of New England. This fact alone indicates that Saye did not see the Massachusetts Bay Colony as God's only elect place for the church. In May of 1640, Winthrop noted in his journal his distress over reports that Lord Saye had been 'disparaging this country' and promoting settlement elsewhere. As Winthrop watched colonists abandon New England for the West Indies he felt betrayed and feared God's judgement. Winthrop wrote to Saye to show him 'how evident it was, that God had chosen this country to plant his people in and therefore how displeasing it would be to the Lord and dangerous to himself to hinder this work, or to discourage men from supplying us, by abasing the goodness of the country, which he [Saye] never saw, and persuading men, that here was no possibility of subsistence. . ."[9]

Saye answered in July 1640. His reply shows that Winthrop had likened him to one Old Testament troublemaker after another: to the disgruntled critics of Moses and Aaron; to the unfaithful spies who brought back a bad report about Canaan; and to Sanballat and Tobiah who opposed Nehemiah's efforts to rebuild the walls of Jerusalem. Saye bristled at Winthrop's insults and at his threat that divine judgement awaited him for his alleged opposition to the work of God. What matters most for our purposes in this fascinating letter is that Lord Saye accused Winthrop of presumptuously connecting himself and Puritan New England to the kingdom of Israel. Winthrop was wrong for 'assuming . . . that there is the like call from God for your going to that part of America and fixing there, that there was for the Israelites going to the land of promise and fixing there'; wrong for discerning a 'like ground' between Nehemiah's task and the raising up of the Bay Colony; and wrong for imagining that the Puritan plantation was 'as much a work of God as his building Jerusalem'. Saye rejected what he saw as a groundless leap from Israel's circumstances to those of the modern Christian. When God commanded them, the Israelites had had to proceed on faith alone, not on human judgement. But the Puritan colonists had no such direct orders. It had been proper for the ancient Israelites to act on faith alone, Saye warned, but the planters of the Bay Colony had to exercise their reason and weigh 'possibilities' and 'probabilities'. He urged Winthrop to 'use with more care' alleged parallels with Scripture. Colonists were free to exercise their God-given judgement in deciding where to settle and ought not to have their consciences bound by Winthrop's misapplication of the Bible.[10]

Winthrop might also have been aware of the argument made by a Separatist a few years earlier against picturing the colonization movement as the reenactment of what was a completed part of redemptive history. Robert Cushman, though a defender of the right of Englishmen to emigrate to the New World, opposed what he saw as the disturbing tendency among some Christians to think of their intended new home as a new Promised Land. In good Protestant fashion, he upheld the sufficiency of Scripture in matters of faith. He used the doctrine of sufficiency to restrain those who would try to find a divine symmetry between biblical Israel and New England. He began with the problem of biblical hermeneutics, that is, with the right method for interpreting God's Word. While God in times past had revealed his will to his people through miraculous deliverances, 'now the ordinary examples and precepts of the Scriptures, reasonably and rightly understood and applied, must be the voice and word that must call us, press us, and direct us in every action'. The warning he then drew from this principle of relying on the Bible alone to know God's work among his people is striking in the context both of the coming Puritan migration (a much grander affair than the Pilgrims' flight) and of the subsequent history of how the Puritans' sense of divine election has been used to explain, and sometimes justify, the United States' redemptive role in the world. His ideas are compressed, his sentence structure archaic and his wording strange to our ears, but his principles are worth considering in some detail:

> Neither is there any land or possession now, like unto the possession which the Jews had in Canaan, . . . now there is no land of that Sanctimony [that is, no Holy Land set apart], no land so appropriated; none typical [that is, none that can serve as a type for Christians]: much less any that can be said to be given of God to any nation as was Canaan, which they and their seed must dwell in, till God sendeth upon them sword or captivity: but now we are in all places strangers and Pilgrims, travelers and sojourners, most properly, having no dwelling but in this earthen Tabernacle; our dwelling is but a wandering, and our abiding but as a fleeting, and in a word our home

is no where, but in the heavens: in that house not made with hands, whose maker and builder is God, and to which all ascend that love the coming of our Lord Jesus.[11]

A few things stand out in this careful distinction. Though he saw Israel and the Church as part of a single, unified story of redemption, Cushman set up a stark contrast between the ancient Jews and modern Christians in one important respect. His claim was blunt: Since the coming of Christ there is no longer any geographic homeland for the Christian corresponding to the Promised Land for the ancient Jews. There is no earthly Holy Land; there is presently no literal homeland that serves theologically as a type of heaven to come; there is no chosen nation for God's people to inhabit. Consequently, believers on this side of Christ's incarnation live as 'strangers and Pilgrims, travelers and sojourners'. In short, their home is 'no where'. They await their eternal home in heaven. The question now for each Christian, Cushman added, was not where to find an earthly Promised Land but where 'he can live to do most good to others'. Cushman himself voyaged to Plymouth Colony and spent about a month there late in 1621. Emigration, he believed, was lawful – that is, biblical – but for much more mundane reasons than as a quest to build God's Promised Land on earth. One can only wonder what would have happened to the trajectory of American history if something closer to Cushman's political theology had come to characterize the New England soul instead of Winthrop's search for an earthly chosen land for an elect people bound by the terms of a national covenant.

Assuming for the moment that Winthrop really did mean for the 'city upon a hill' to serve as the defining image and rhetorical climax of his discourse, what might he have envisioned that city being or doing in the world? Telling the story of what historians, orators, editors, politicians and pundits did to the metaphor over the next 400 years will occupy the rest of this book. We know from the previous chapter that before the voyage to the New World, Winthrop had talked of the projected colony of the Massachusetts Bay Company as a 'shelter and a hiding place' and a 'place of refuge'.

Now it is possible that a place of refuge could also serve simultaneously as an example of a godly commonwealth to England and beyond or even as the GHQ for world reformation. One identity does not necessarily preclude others. An exemplary city could also have a mission of global transformation. In the text of the Model of Christian Charity, Winthrop clearly hoped that the Massachusetts Bay Colony would become an example for later plantations. He envisioned 'succeeding plantations' saying of themselves, may 'the Lord make it like that of New England'. By being a 'city upon a hill', his very next words, New England would serve as a beacon for such colonies, a beacon to guide and to warn. How expansive Winthrop's vision was for those 'succeeding plantations' is hard to say. Did he picture a constellation of Puritan plantations in New England or did he imagine something on a grander scale? In any case, the 'eyes of all people' would be upon this 'city upon a hill'. Winthrop never instructed the colonists to *build* a city upon a hill in the New World, a point missed by countless commentators. Winthrop warned them that *as* a city on a hill they would have to take care to fulfill their special commission before a watching world. Even if they failed miserably, they would still be a city upon a hill. There was no escaping that destiny. There was no avoiding being a spectacle to the world.

The story of the building of the Massachusetts Bay Colony after Winthrop's landing in June of 1630 belongs to other books and authors. It has been told many times and by some of America's most gifted historians. It will be told again. It is one part of the story of what America is, what it was and what it never became. Now that we have met a less familiar city on a hill, we are ready to trace the story of the metaphor from Winthrop's Model of Christian Charity into the history books and from the history books into American politics and the nation's civil religion.

But first came 208 years of silence.

3

A land of light, 1630–1838

We are a city set on an hill, and the honor of God doth greatly depend on our behavior.
JONATHAN EDWARDS, 1737

The civilization of New England has been like a beacon lit upon mountain tops which, after warming all in its vicinity, casts a glow over the distant horizon.
ALEXIS DE TOCQUEVILLE, 1835

No evidence survives of any preacher, politician, historian or member of the general public quoting from the Model of Christian Charity before 1838 and hardly any before 1858. For two centuries after 1630, no American had yet elevated Winthrop's discourse to its canonical status at the head of the American Scripture. No one had yet read it as a prophecy of America's future greatness. No one had yet incorporated its cadences into the American civil religion. No one had yet used it to anchor American exceptionalism, to plot the trajectory of US foreign policy, or to map America's mission and destiny. By the mid-nineteenth century, the metaphor of the city on a hill had no fixed association yet in the public mind with John Winthrop or his meditations on mercy. No such association was possible while the discourse remained nearly forgotten among the Winthrop family papers. In those 200 years of obscurity, the Model served no one as a storehouse of metaphors for the national myth.

The question of what happened to the *city on a hill* between 1630 and 1838 is different from the question of what happened to the Model of Christian Charity. These two centuries were 'silent' only for the Model and not for the biblical metaphor of the city. The city on a hill, along with such closely associated images as 'light', 'candlestick', and 'beacon' and the conviction that 'the eyes of the world' were upon the American experiment, continued to be used by preachers in their weekly sermons; by Puritans other than Winthrop in renewed summonses to covenantal obligations; by eminent eighteenth-century divines in elaborations of the national covenant; and by such celebrated foreign observers as Alexis de Tocqueville, the French historian, sociologist and political theorist.

Before proceeding in our search for the city on a hill, we need to recognize a way in which the Puritan settlers of New England were unexceptional. Rather than innovate in their use of Matthew 5.14, they brought with them a long-standing habit of referring to godly communities as a city on a hill. The same thing was true of the metaphor of the Puritan colonies as a 'New Israel'. John Winthrop did nothing radically new by quoting Matthew 5.14 in the context he did and applying it to the Puritan refugees headed for New England. And there is no reason at all to assume that when other statesmen and preachers used the same biblical metaphor they were necessarily quoting Winthrop. Winthrop and other Puritans drew on an existing practice, well established at least a century before. They acted as points of transmission in the history of the metaphor and not as points of origin. They continued an existing practice rather than inventing something new or uniquely American. This is just one small example, incidentally, of how the seemingly endless search for the 'Puritan origins' of anything and everything in American history gets the question wrong by failing to reach back behind the first settlements to consider the broader English and European context.

English Puritans in the sixteenth and seventeenth centuries used the image of a city on a hill to honour exemplary churches and to designate godly communities worthy of emulation. Winthrop biographer Francis Bremer cites the example of one leader who compared Colchester – a town about ten miles south of Winthrop's manor at Groton – under the persecutions of Mary Tudor to 'the city upon a hill'.[1] Likewise, a Baptist elder, recounting religious oppression under the Stuarts, praised the pious dissenters at Bristol 'as a Citty upon a Hill that could not be hid'.[2] In 1638, Lord Saye, despite his sharp rebuke of Winthrop two years later for his mishandling of biblical typology, warned John Cotton, by then in New England, that the devil would scheme to discredit God's work. In view of Satan's attempts to divide the Puritan community, 'it behooveth you in that place who are a city set upon a hill to use all means to prevent his slights and subtleties'.[3] And in John Milton's judgement in 1641, England herself once held such an esteemed place at the forefront of God's work of Reformation that it had been privileged 'to be the first that should set up a standard for the recovery of lost truth, and blow the first evangelic trumpet to the nations, holding up, as from a hill, the new lamp of saving light to all Christendom'.[4]

New England continued the practice. Two prominent early Puritan settlers, Peter Bulkeley and Edward Johnson, stand out in this regard. Ironically, though these authors' names are now unfamiliar to most Americans, their books were in print in the seventeenth century and used frequently as sources for early colonial history. Bulkeley and Johnson became standard authorities on the early settlement of New England while Winthrop's Model remained unknown. If anyone bothered to notice that the early Puritans used the city on a hill to describe New England, these two figures would have been the ones to turn to.

The Reverend Peter Bulkeley came to New England in 1635 with his family and helped found the town of Concord and to 'gather' the church there. The Cambridge-educated Bulkeley had served as rector of All Saints church in the village of Odell, Bedfordshire, since 1610. His most famous descendant was Ralph Waldo Emerson. Bulkeley's nonconformity put him at odds with

Archbishop William Laud, and he joined the increasing number of Puritans who fled England in the 1630s. Twice in a collection of sermons preached in Concord and published in 1646 as the *Gospel Covenant*, Bulkeley described New England as a 'city on a hill'.[5] Near the beginning of what grew into an extended set of reflections on the theology of grace and works, Bulkeley addressed a personified New England. He did so in terms familiar to us today from Winthrop's 1630 discourse and consistent with the wider Puritan framework of the national covenant of spiritual and temporal blessing and cursing.

The Concord pastor warned that New England, as the recipient of greater privileges from the hand of God, would be held to greater accountability. The formula was simple and often repeated in his day. Among these blessings were an unhindered gospel and the faithful preaching of godly pastors. That favoured and exposed position brought with it great danger – the certainty of divine retribution visited upon a community that failed to 'walk worthy of the means of thy salvation'. 'The Lord looks for more from thee than from other people', Bulkeley warned his flock, in particular 'more zeal for God, more love to his truth, more justice and equity in thy ways. . . .' New Englanders were nothing less than 'a special people, an only people' – indeed, there was 'none like thee in all the earth'. As had been the case for Winthrop's shipmates, this was a fearful position in which to be placed.

In these passages, we sense again the awesome weight of responsibility hanging over New England as a spectacle to the world. Combining verses from the book of Revelation, the prophet Isaiah and the gospel of Matthew, Bulkeley impressed upon his fellow New Englanders their urgent need to honour both the Word of God and God's preachers, 'lest for neglect of either, God remove thy candlestick out of the midst of thee; lest being now as a City upon an hill, which many seek unto, thou be left like a beacon on the top of a mountain, desolate and forsaken'. Early in the book of Revelation, the Apostle John depicted the churches of Asia Minor as seven candlesticks (in the rendering of the Geneva Bible). John conveyed Jesus' stern rebuke to the wayward church at Ephesus 'to repent and do the first works or else I will come against thee shortly, and will remove thy candlestick out of his place, except thou amend'. To the word 'candlestick', the Geneva annotations added an explanation familiar from the long tradition of biblical commentary: 'The office of pastor is compared to a candlestick or lamp for as much as he ought to shine before men'. Bulkeley applied these verses from the Apocalypse to the community as a whole and not just to pastors. And he immediately added the city on a hill from Matthew 5 and then the vivid warning to rebellious Israel found in Isaiah 30.7: God's chosen people would be 'left as a ship mast upon the top of a mountain and as a beacon upon a hill' – a terrible fate awaiting an ungrateful, unworthy people. 'Be instructed, and take heed', he added ominously.

Bulkeley returned to the city metaphor at the end of the *Gospel Covenant* to reiterate his warning to his Concord community not to become the wrong kind of spectacle to the world. The context was God's call to holiness: 'And for ourselves here, the people of New England, we should in a special manner labor to shine forth in holiness above other people; we have that plenty and abundance of ordinances and means of grace, as few people enjoy the like; we are as a City set upon a hill, in the open view of all the earth; the eyes of the world are upon us, because we profess ourselves to be a people in Covenant with God, and therefore not only the Lord our God, with whom we have made Covenant, but heaven and earth, angels and men, that are witnesses of our profession, will cry shame upon us, if we walk contrary to the Covenant which we have professed and promised to walk in. If we open the mouths of men against our profession, by reason of the scandalousness of our lives, we (of all men) shall have the greater sin'. The similarities here to Winthrop's Model are striking and go far beyond the metaphor of the city on a hill. Clearly, Bulkeley and Winthrop relied on a common method of biblical interpretation and application: they exhibit the same tendency to impose God's standard for

Israel on the earthly polity, the same emphasis on the purity of the ordinances, and the same prospect of shame awaiting the covenant community that disobeyed God.

Edward Johnson, a Puritan layman from Kent, arrived in the New World in 1636. His *Wonder-Working Providence of Sion's Saviour in New England*, the first history of the settlement (published in London in 1653), used the metaphor of the city retrospectively to describe the zealous early days of New England 20 years before. Johnson cited Matthew 5.14 only indirectly, but his context reinforces the pattern of the metaphor's primary role as a warning, in this case to the people of New England to use their rare liberty to choose their own church leaders well and exercise proper church discipline. As Congregational churches, they had unprecedented 'liberty' and 'responsibility' to observe God's ordinances according to his revealed will. They had to help guard the doctrine and practice of the church. 'Let your profession outstrip your confession, for seeing you are to be set as lights upon a Hill more obvious than the highest mountain in the world, keep close to Christ that you may shine full of his glory, who implores you, and grub not continually in the earth, like blind moles, but by your amiable conversation seek the winning of many to your Master's service'.[6]

This sampling from only two first-generation Puritan authors helps us to hear Winthrop's Model of Christian Charity as part of a larger and sustained effort to tell the Puritan settlers who they were in God's plan and what the stakes were for their project in the New World. They used the metaphor of the city on a hill along with other familiar biblical images to articulate the meaning of New England in a knowable redemptive history unfolding in their own day and before their eyes. Over the next few decades, the constant lament from second- and third-generation preachers in their jeremiads was the people's failure to obey the terms of the national covenant. They fell into self-love, the idolatry of wealth and material pleasures, Sabbath-breaking, and other sins. Consequently, they suffered God's heavy hand of chastisement on their communities. His wrath broke out against them in poor crops, natural disasters, famine, sickness and Indian raids. But they never doubted their chosenness, only their righteousness as God's elect nation. In shameful contrast to their own disobedience, the heroic first generation became the standard of covenantal obedience, the mark they missed. Later Puritans such as the prolific and influential Cotton Mather extolled Winthrop as 'the father of New-England'. Ancient Greece had her Lycurgus and Rome her Numa, but New England had her Winthrop, a man possessed of their virtues but devoid of their vices, a Moses who had led the 'chosen people' through the 'American wilderness'. Mather elevated Winthrop as an 'example well-worthy to be copied' and 'greatly imitable'. He called him 'our New-England Nehemiah' who skillfully administered 'our American Jerusalem'. In his wise and judicious statesmanship he was an American Joseph.[7] For Mather and those who turned to his books as sources of sacred history, the first generation became a set of exemplary figures, models of Christian doctrine and life.

Many elements of the American myth as God's New Israel were already present in Mather at the beginning of the eighteenth century. And they appeared independently of the metaphor of the city on a hill. Mather never applied Matthew 5.14 to British North America. He never quoted from the Model of Christian Charity even though he had at least some of Winthrop's papers at his disposal and quoted from Winthrop's journal, including the famous 'Little Speech' on liberty. Mather would become a key source for later historians' knowledge of the early days of the Puritan colonies. But the Model's obscurity continued into the eighteenth century.

Thirty years later, in the era of the celebrated evangelists George Whitefield and John and Charles Wesley, New England's most prominent preacher, theologian and philosopher wrestled with what it meant for his people to be a city on a hill. In some ways, Jonathan Edwards' theological reflections on Jesus' metaphor constitute a bypath in the story of how America became the city on a hill. Edwards contributed to the making of the national myth, but that role went largely unnoticed until recently. His millennial expectations for America as the probable seat of Christ's kingdom have generated considerable debate among scholars. But the narrower question of how he interpreted and applied Matthew 5.14 is less well known and potentially more significant. Extracting his views on one part of one verse in the New Testament is not the way to understand fully such a towering and complex figure as Edwards. But doing so reveals a great deal about how one influential preacher used the metaphor to perpetuate the New England idea of the national covenant. Edwards' preaching makes it possible to take a sounding, as it were, exactly half way between Winthrop's landing in the New World and the publication of his discourse in 1838. Edwards did not have and did not need Winthrop's help in this task. He developed his understanding of the city on a hill independently of anything Winthrop wrote in the Model of Christian Charity, but he spoke out of a shared tradition and carried that habit of mind forward in a way the Puritan governor and the early generations of settlers would have recognized.

After graduating from Yale, Edwards followed his grandfather, Solomon Stoddard, as pastor of the large Congregational church in Northampton, Massachusetts, a position he held from 1726 until the increasingly controversial minister left in 1751 for a new call in Stockbridge. Edwards achieved international fame as a leader in the revival movement that swept through British North America in 1734 and 1735, a series of events later called the 'Great Awakening'. Word of the revival spread to England and beyond thanks to the publication in 1738 of Edwards' *Faithful Narrative of the Surprising Work of God*. A prolific author, Edwards established himself as one of the most influential public figures in eighteenth-century America, a stature testified to by his appointment as president of Princeton just before his untimely death in 1758.

In a series of sermons preached in the aftermath of his congregation's intense awakening in the mid-1730s, Edwards handled the metaphor of the city on a hill in ways familiar from his Puritan ancestors but also bearing his unique stamp. His use of Jesus' metaphor for the church and its teaching ministry points to some enduring features of New Englanders' self-understanding, including the powerful narrative in which they pictured themselves playing a starring role, whether triumphant or tragic.[8] The half-dozen sermons Edwards preached in the 1730s that touched in some way on the city on a hill provide abundant evidence for the Northampton pastor's characteristic way of approaching the metaphor.[9] The occasion for some of these sermons was a public fast day. Like his Puritan ancestors before him and any New England preacher of his own day, Edwards delivered fast-day and thanksgiving sermons in addition to his weekly Sunday homilies. In these occasional addresses, he filled a very visible public role within the community in times of natural disaster, war and other earthly trials. He was expected to find meaning for these events within the biblical narrative and within the theology of a national covenant. Like an Old Testament prophet addressing God's wayward people, Edwards warned, rebuked, called to repentance, and promised deliverance and restoration to his Northampton community. In the judgement of historian Harry Stout, this genre of sermon makes it clear 'that Edwards, together with his rationalist counterparts, approached New England as a 'peculiar' nation who, like Israel of old, enjoyed a special covenant relationship with God'.[10] Even sermons Edwards delivered from the pulpit on Sundays may have reflected this same tendency, though he did not always date his sermons and when he did, he often gave only the month and year, making it difficult to know when he preached them.

Historian Gerald McDermott has drawn attention to Edwards' idea of a 'professing community'. That idea provides one important insight into why he handled the metaphor of the city as he did. In Edwards' theology, any community that entered into a Covenant with God for a special work and experienced special divine blessings and responsibility because of that relationship, constituted such a society. As his preaching in the 1730s made clear, Edwards understood British North America in general, Puritan New England a bit closer to home, and his own town of Northampton most immediately as 'professing communities' exposed to the eyes of the world. Exactly why they achieved this status (or had it thrust upon them) and what were the implications of that identity unfolded in several of the sermons Edwards preached following the tumultuous revival in Northampton.

In a sermon dated July 1736, taking Matthew 5.14 as its text, Edwards offered his fullest explication of the meaning of Jesus' metaphor. As was his custom, he moved from the biblical text to the doctrine built on that text and then to the application for his own flock – the pattern taught long before by William Perkins and manifest in Winthrop's discourse. Often, Edwards's application of a text became the longest and most elaborate part of his sermon. Generations of Puritan preachers had done the same. In this instance, he began with a fairly standard interpretation of Jesus' words. Jesus primarily addressed his disciples as a city on a hill, and also more generally his church – a handling of the text consistent with John Calvin's reading of it and in line with the Church Fathers, as we saw in Chapter Two. What Jesus promised his disciples during his earthly ministry found fulfillment most immediately in the book of Acts, Edwards explained. 'The church then was in a remarkable manner as a city set on an hill.'[11] And throughout the subsequent ages, this calling had remained the church's identity and burden.

There was nothing particularly notable in the way Edwards began. But he then expanded the city on a hill beyond the church at large to denote any 'professing society' – any Christian community, that is, whose faith or behaviour 'distinguishes' it and causes it to be spoken of 'far and near'. That reputation could come in the way it had to the first disciples when they boldly preached the 'foolishness' of the gospel to unbelievers. Or it could come to a community distinguished by the fervour of its profession. Moreover, such a community might also have benefitted from 'remarkable works' of God among its members comparable to God delivering the Israelites from bondage and defeating their enemies, or his miraculous provision for the church at its founding, or some other extraordinary blessing. Furthermore, a city on a hill may have earned that distinction not only for its fame or for the blessings it received but also for the remarkable influence it had on others.[12]

Edwards multiplied and emphasized these ways of being 'distinguished' in order to drive to his main point that a community 'set up' in this way before the eyes of the world carried a 'great obligation'. The burden of being a city on a hill preoccupied Edwards. God's special blessing meant special obligation— the same covenantal logic present in Winthrop, Bulkeley, and Johnson a century before. As a spectacle to the world, a city on a hill risked dishonouring its calling by any inconsistency in doctrine or life. As Jesus said in the context of the city metaphor, they were called to be a light to the world through their good works. Conspicuous to such a degree, they were capable of 'more good' and 'more hurt'. These warnings are hardly distinguishable from the words Peter Bulkeley preached to his congregation: 'If we open the mouths of men against our profession, by reason of the scandalousness of our lives, we (of all men) shall have the greater sin'.

The contrast between Edwards and his ancestors has more to do with differences of degree than kind. The Northampton pastor did not do anything new to the metaphor by applying Jesus' teaching to an earthly community. But the sheer repetition, emotional intensity and urgency of his demands for covenantal obedience distinguishes Edwards's preaching. He placed a tremendous weight of responsibility on God's chosen people in New England. It is not likely that Edwards would have thought that he was applying Matthew 5.14 to something or someone other than the church and Christians. There was no clear line for him between church and community. Any notion of a distinction between the 'secular' city of Northampton and the 'sacred' body of the church would have struck him as artificial. He taught a national covenant of works right alongside a covenant of grace and the evangelical 'new birth'. This mixture is one of the challenges facing a modern reader trying to understand Edwards and, by extension, trying to grasp the logic in this potent way of reading the meaning of America. God still dealt with nations in modern times as he had in the Old Testament. God still dealt with professing peoples as he had with Israel.

Edwards's use of the phrase 'professing people' here and elsewhere raises the important question of who exactly constituted the 'people' in his sermons. His fluid movement from ancient Israel, to the church across the ages, and then to America and the town of Northampton, required, especially in that last theological migration, a temporal identity for God's 'people' that might seem less obvious to later Americans than it had been to Edwards and his congregation – at least to later Americans, including Christians, who doubted their nation's parallel to ancient Israel. Moving so effortlessly from biblical texts to the New England context required that statesmen and preachers make little to no distinction between Old Testament Israel as God's chosen people and a current settlement of Christians in the New World or between the New Testament Church as God's chosen people and these same earthly communities. Throughout the seventeenth and eighteenth centuries, preachers stressed the parallels between Israel and their own time and place. They commonly spoke of their own land 'acting over again' the pattern of covenantal disobedience seen among the Hebrews. That identity, which at times seemed almost inter-changeable, meant that the words God addressed to his people Israel he also addressed to the villages of New England. The connection between the two, evident in countless sermons and speeches, may sound odd to modern ears, but it was accepted as a first principle of life together in New England. This was how God worked, then and now. This is who the people of New England were. As Edwards would tell his congregation in 1737, 'There is perhaps no people now on the face of the earth whose case has been so parallel with that of the Israelites as ours has'.[13] And that similarity brought with it good news and bad.

It should come as no surprise that Edwards thought about his Northampton congregation within this framework. The town was the very sort of 'distinguished' society set apart by God and appropriately designated a 'city on a hill'. In Northampton's case, that identity derived directly from the intense religious revivals that Northampton experienced and Edwards defended and publicized in 1734–1735. He feared that his own city on a hill would fall under greater scrutiny and therefore under greater divine condemnation (including temporal punishments visited upon individuals and the town) if it failed to live up to its profession. As word of the spiritual stirring in Northampton had reached other colonies and across the Atlantic to London, Edwards reported, it seemed that the eyes of the world had indeed fastened upon his congregation. They ought therefore to take care to lead lives marked by moral rectitude, civic harmony, just government, generosity, well-ordered households and the rearing of godly youth. Northampton was exceptional in the degree to which it enjoyed God's gracious blessing during the awakening; therefore a greater burden of responsibility lay upon its shoulders and a greater judgement would befall it if its practice did not match its profession. And that judgement could include temporal punishment.

Edwards left no doubt about all this as he moved into his sermon's long application that summer of 1736. 'This town', he said of Northampton, 'is in a remarkable degree such a society, as is spoken of in the text and doctrine. It has been so in a considerable degree formerly. It has in time past been a town of an higher profession, and more noted, for the works which God had wrought in it than most towns, if not than any town in the land. But it is become more remarkably so of late, by means of the late wonderful pouring out of the Spirit of God upon us. God has hereby set us up on high to the view and observation of the world. We are as a city set upon an hill, in all those ways that have been mentioned'. Edwards piled warning on top of warning. Northampton was so singularly favoured by God 'that there probably never was any town in this land, under so great obligations of that kind mentioned in the text and doctrine, to honor their profession by their practice as this town'.[14]

Throughout the following spring of 1737, as Edwards's thoughts returned often to the city on a hill, he repeated his warnings, and seemed to come closer and closer to convicting Northampton of having abandoned its covenant obligations. Back in 1630, John Winthrop, operating within a similar covenantal framework, had immediately followed his invocation of the city on a hill, by warning, 'If we shall deal falsely with our God in this work we have undertaken and so cause him to withdraw his present help from us, we shall be made a story and a by-word throughout the world'. Now Edwards seemed on the verge of telling his congregation that they had indeed dealt falsely with their God. In a fast-day sermon in March on Ezekiel, he warned, 'If we think to escape divine judgments as much as other people, with living no better than other people, we are much mistaken. No such thing is to be expected. We are a city set on an hill, and the honor of God doth greatly depend on our behavior'.[15]

So close was the association in Edwards's mind between Matthew 5.14 and judgement that he seemed rarely to have used the city on a hill apart from such warnings. Indeed, the metaphor became closely tied to the type of narrative of decline known to generations of Puritans in their preacher's jeremiads. This story required an exemplary generation of 'forefathers' standing at the founding. They provided the benchmark. In a second fast-day sermon, in March 1737, Edwards wove into a powerful rebuke the three elements of New England as a 'covenant people', the narrative of decline, and the heroic stature of the first generation. His preoccupation with the fearsome implications of being a city on a hill pulsed through the sermon, though he never used the precise metaphor this time. He contrasted New England's privileged identity as a 'land of light' with its current spiritual backsliding. 'Hence learn what great cause we have to lament the degeneration and corruption of the land', he complained. His repeated use of the word 'distinguished' – three times in three sentences – echoed his earlier designation of a 'professing people' as a city on a hill: 'We have been greatly distinguished by God as a covenant people. God has distinguished us by making known his covenant to us. We have been in a very distinguishing manner a land of light'. Before the first settlers came, 'this land was once a land of darkness – full [of] habitations of cruelty'. But thanks to the gospel, there was 'now scarce any land in the world that has enjoyed greater light'. 'The land of our forefathers has been a land [of] great light', he continued, 'but there has been more of a mixture of dark with light'. That darkness, Edwards explained, came in the activity of the Papacy in North America, the neglect of the purity of God's ordinances, and the rise of the heresies of Socinianism and Arminianism.[16]

Two months later, Northampton's identity as a city on a hill was still very much on Edwards' mind as he fretted over the town's worsening sin and discord. The sweet days of revival, enjoyed so recently, now seemed long over. In a sermon in May 1737 on 2 Samuel 20.19 he reminded his congregation once again that they were on display in America and abroad. Ministers in England had expressed 'their great joy, and their design to spread the narrative of [the revival] in the world, as much as in 'em lies'. A watching world expected more 'glad tidings', but sadly it would now hear that 'our mouths have been filled with backbitings'. And here followed the warning to a contentious and fractious community, a distant echo of Lord Saye's warning to John Cotton: 'No town in America [is] so like a city set on an hill [by God], and to whom he has, in so great a degree, betrusted the honor of religion. [God has] committed the honor of his own great name by putting honor upon us, and by [the] blessings bestowed on us'.[17] But that honour was about to turn to shame.

Edwards developed his lament over the backsliding city most elaborately a year later in April 1738 in another fast-day sermon. Choosing Jeremiah 2.5 as his text, he preached a modern jeremiad against his modern Israel. He shared the Old Testament prophet's distress that the covenant people had dared to find fault with God for what were in fact the consequences of their own sin. Edwards applied the narrative of Israel's decline first to America ('this land') and then more particularly to Northampton ('this town').[18] His wielding of this text against America and Northampton brings us back to a few basic assumptions that by now have become clearer: 1) God enters into (and has entered into) national covenants in times and places and with peoples other than ancient Israel; 2) the responsibilities of that covenant are known and capable of being obeyed; 3) obedience to the national covenant brings blessings while 'backsliding' brings curses, including temporal punishment; and 4) a covenantal community's infidelity potentially brings shame on the whole work of God in the world. If America and Northampton were not covenant peoples like national Israel, then Edwards's application of Jeremiah's indictment to the earthly communities of his day would not have any theological grounding. The pattern we encountered in Winthrop's thought as he put pen to paper aboard the *Arbella* endured in Edwards a century later, namely, the Puritan determination to 're-Israelize' the church into a literal, temporal people occupying a literal, geographic land.

Edwards himself made this point explicit as he continued his April 1738 sermon. British North America was founded as a 'covenant people', he claimed, and not just any covenant people but one set up 'in a special manner' similar to Israel. The alleged parallels had been familiar to generations of New Englanders. God had called out the first settlers by delivering them from their 'heavy yoke of bondage' in England. He had carried them over the wilderness of the Atlantic Ocean. He had made them 'a peculiar people to himself', emptied the land of its 'heathen' inhabitants, blessed them with the liberty to observe 'his word and ordinances', and sealed a covenant with them. America was not the modern day's only professing community of Christians, Edwards conceded, but it was certainly exceptional in the degree to which its own story matched Israel's: 'There is probably no people in the world, whose case in the manner of our becoming a distinct covenant people, is so parallel with that of the church of Israel as this people'.[19]

Having mapped out the origin of the professing people, Edwards then extolled the heroic founding generation's exemplary fidelity to their Covenant with God. He prepared his listeners for the coming contrast between the purity of 'those times' and their own debased generation by artfully repeating the word 'then': 'then the land in general was pure in the doctrines professed in it'; 'then also the land in general was pure in its worship'; 'then a spirit of love prevailed amongst Christians'; and so on. These were the very things Winthrop had aspired to inculcate in the Model of Christian Charity. As in Mather, the fathers retained their mythic standing as the measure of spiritual infidelity and covenantal decline.

Since that glorious founding, Edwards regretted, America had allowed heresy to flourish, had grown lax in the 'work of conversion and experimental piety' and content with 'mere form' in religion, and had indulged in 'drunkenness, profane swearing, lasciviousness . . . and all manner of debauchery'. It was a short step from this indictment of the American colonies as a whole to Northampton. And this is the familiar scenario where Edwards concluded his sermon. His own community had been the beneficiary of a great outpouring of God's Spirit just three years before. In light of such blessing, its declension brought greater judgement. Great was the blessing and great was the departure. In the awakening, 'He has distinguished us as a people especially favored of the Lord. The fame of what [he] hath done for us, hath reached far and wide, and we are looked upon by God's people, at a great distance, as an happy people'. Despite their backsliding, God had continued to be gracious to them and spared them from one calamity after another, preferring in His goodness to deal gently with them. But the risk remained that the covenant people would deal falsely with their God. Like their Puritan ancestors, they still lived on that precarious knife's edge of covenantal obedience and divine wrath. And in all of this, Edwards' thoughts were not far from the city on a hill. 'Let it be considered that our thus casting such a reflection on God, is the way to bring shame and disgrace on ourselves. We are as a city set on an hill. We have made a high profession of religion, and the eyes of the world are upon us to observe'.[20] Northampton might lose its blessing and cover itself in shame, but through it all it would never stop being a city on a hill.

A fuller understanding of Edwards's role in making Jesus' metaphor into an American myth would take us into his eschatology, his expectation that America might be the site of the coming of Christ's millennial kingdom, his view of history as the outworking of the conflict between the Papacy and the Reformation, and the nuances of his theology of church and state. Among these larger questions, one historical debate has centered on the degree to which Edwards promoted what historian Ernest Lee Tuveson in the 1960s called America's 'Redeemer Myth'. Tuveson himself emphasized Edwards's expectation of an earthly millennium. A decade later, Sacvan Bercovitch reinforced Edwards's contribution to America's sense of mission and of itself as the principal agent in sacred history. Similarly, Harry Stout ended his study of Edwards's relationship to his Puritan ancestors by concluding, 'The vision of a redeemer nation and a covenant people was dazzling, and none, including Edwards, could escape its glare. As one voice among thousands, Edwards helped perpetuate that quintessentially Puritan notion of a righteous city set high upon a hill for all the world to see'. More recently, Gerald McDermott has tried to bring out Edwards's more 'pessimistic' view of America and, correctly, as we have seen, the Northampton pastor's insistence that his town had become a negative example to the world – a city of shame, not a shining beacon of righteousness.[21] Edwards's urgent pleadings to his congregation were far too sober to be read as self-congratulatory progenitors of the myth of the 'redeemer nation'.

But even with McDermott's correction in mind, one thing about Edwards remains clear: whether righteous or unrighteous, obedient or disobedient, New Englanders were God's chosen people, a spectacle to the world. Either way, the covenantal relationship was real and inescapable. America could not be hidden. Its light may have grown dim, but the city on a hill – even as just one city on a hill among many possible cities – laboured under the duties of a national covenant of works. This view may indeed be 'pessimistic', but it does nothing to affect America's standing as a city on a hill and how that theology can affect the nation's understanding of the church and its calling in the world. A more nuanced 'Edwardsian' handling of the metaphor might make for a more chastened national identity, or a more restrained foreign policy, or a more communitarian theory of social justice, but it would still be premised on an identification of America as 'our Israel' and open the way for all the implications of national chosenness. Edwards used the metaphor of the city to bind his church members with the cords of a national covenant, obscuring the Augustinian understanding of a sojourning City of God on pilgrimage through the City of Man. Better known, his sermons might have restrained American conduct with a sobering sense of divine accountability. But like so many of his era, he blurred the sacred and the secular. The things of Caesar looked very much like the things of God from inside the walls of Edwards's city.

Beyond his mixing of kingdoms, Edwards repeatedly resorted to a narrative of decline, a habit of mind demonstrating that, since the days of the earliest Puritan settlements and through the eighteenth century, America's identity as a chosen people, as a city on a hill, never had to be tied to a narrative of 'rising glory' and inevitable material and moral progress. The Puritans knew that a 'shining' city does not always shine. It can earn a reputation for disobedience and shame and still be very much a city on a hill the way Winthrop, Bulkeley, and Edwards feared – a city under judgement, a city that had become a spectacle of folly instead of divine blessing. Later, the metaphor of the city on a hill became entwined with the triumphant narrative of national greatness, but this was not so originally. As the metaphor was remade from biblical metaphor into national myth, it retained much of its sense of judgement. It retained enough of the traditional biblical identity that the metaphor's new use did not yet eclipse the earlier warnings. New England's status as God's 'peculiar people' brought with it ominous covenant obligations, higher accountability, and thus greater judgement for failure. The possibility, if not the likelihood, of backsliding is built into this story. A narrative of decline is every bit as much a part of the chosen-people identity as the narrative of progress. They derive from the same theology of a national covenant. The idea of the 'redeemer nation' and the narrative of decline could and did fit comfortably together – whether in Winthrop's Boston, Edwards's Northampton, or twenty-first century America. The original Puritan narrative does not present us with a choice between a hubristic 'redeemer myth' and a more modest 'suffering servant'. These grew together out of the chosen-people habit of mind. To the degree that Edwards encouraged that habit of mind, he helped unmake the biblical metaphor.

As Edwards makes clear, without the publication of the Model of Christian Charity the metaphor of the city on a hill remained available right where it had been for 1,600 years: in the midst of Jesus' Sermon on the Mount. The world was not waiting for the rediscovery of Winthrop's Model to make the city on a hill famous. Or at least the church was not waiting. Christian ministers continued to cite Matthew 5.14 in countless ordinary sermons, and they did so in ways that never became part of the story of *America* as the city on a hill because they continued in unspectacular ways to apply the metaphor to the *church* as the city on a hill. Some, like Edwards, might stretch the metaphor and apply it to earthly communities beyond the strict limits of the church. Some might even, in election-day sermons and on similar occasions, address godly magistrates as 'a city set upon a hill', as Congregationalist Samuel McClintock did in 1784.[22] But on countless other unremarked and unremarkable occasions, the metaphor of the city on a hill remained in the possession of the church and continued to speak Jesus' words of warning to his disciples to watch their doctrine and life.

Occasionally, but less often than the metaphor's modern ubiquity has led us to expect, orators, politicians and preachers from the seventeenth through the nineteenth century used the city on a hill and closely related images to describe America. In March of 1780, for instance, Massachusetts patriot John

Adams found Jesus' words from the Sermon on the Mount an apt metaphor
for what the American cause looked like from Europe. Engaged in his diplo-
matic mission to Paris at the time, the Unitarian Adams wrote a word of
encouragement to General Nathanael Greene:

> Every operation of your army has its influence upon all the powers of
> Europe in France, Spain, England, Ireland, Holland, Sweden, Denmark,
> Russia, Prussia, Portugal, and even in the German Empire.
>
> America is the city set upon a hill. I do not think myself guilty of exagger-
> ation, vanity or presumption, when I say, that the proceedings of Congress
> are more attended to than those of any court in Europe, and the motions of
> our armies than any of theirs. And there are more political lies made and
> circulated about both than all the rest: which renders genuine intelligence,
> from good authority, the more interesting and important.[23]

Adams's use of the city on a hill to describe America's conspicuous role in the
world in 1780, though a rare instance among his generation, indicates the
metaphor's ongoing usefulness while the Model of Christian Charity remained
out of sight and out of mind. Significantly, being such a spectacle to the world
rendered the Continental Congress and the army the victims of damaging
'political lies' in Europe's capitals. America's status made it vulnerable to abuse,
not exempt from the world's ills.

Astute foreign observers of the young United States in the decades ahead
echoed, and at times affirmed, the Puritan descendants' consciousness of their
unique contribution to American civilization. Alexis de Tocqueville wrote
about Winthrop and the Puritans in his celebrated *Democracy in America*, the
first volume of which appeared in 1835.[24] Almost immediately Tocqueville
took up the question of the origin of Anglo-American political ideals and
institutions. He went back in search of that 'point of departure' from which
America's character traits emerged. He began with the Jamestown colony in

Virginia, but turned quickly to the early settlements of New England in his quest to find the key to modern America. 'It is in these English colonies of the North', he wrote, '. . . that were brought together the two or three main ideas which today constitute the social theory of the United States'. And those 'two or three main ideas' Tocqueville soon identified as freedom of worship wedded to an unprecedented degree of political self-government. These ideas, at the time 'unknown or neglected by European nations', took hold in New England, 'the future symbol of a great nation'.

The appendix to volume one indicates the sources Tocqueville relied on most heavily for estimating New England's significance to America and the world. He singled out for praise Nathaniel Morton's *New England's Memorial*, Governor Thomas Hutchinson's *History of the Colony of Massachusetts*, Cotton Mather's *Magnalia Christi Americana*, and the series of *Collections* published by the Massachusetts Historical Society beginning in 1792 and continuing in Tocqueville's own time. Had the Frenchman visited America just a few years later, he likely would have known about Winthrop's Model of Christian Charity. As it was, he seemed to know Winthrop secondhand and largely through Mather's *Magnalia*. He quoted a section from Winthrop's so-called 'Little Speech on Liberty' that he found in Mather as an example of the development of the idea and institutions of political freedom in England's North American colonies.

Tocqueville had a good ear, and from these early histories he picked up more than a little of the tone and language of the early seventeenth-century Puritans. In fact, he sounded like someone paraphrasing Winthrop in exactly the way Americans have come to expect. 'The New England principles spread first of all to neighboring states; subsequently, they reached successively the more distant, ending up, if I may put it this way, by *permeating* the entire confederation. Now they exert their influence beyond its limits to the whole American world. The civilization of New England has been like a beacon lit upon mountain tops which, after warming all in its vicinity, casts a glow over the distant horizon'. 'The founding of New England', he continued, 'was a novel spectacle and everything attending it was unusual and original'.

Prominent Americans in the nineteenth century also continued to use Jesus' metaphor from time to time either to praise or admonish their cities, states and nation. Public speakers elevated Boston, New York, Baltimore and other growing metropolises to such eminence. In 1845, for instance, Robert C. Winthrop, a direct descendant of the Puritan governor and a man we will return to later, called Boston 'a city set on a hill' in a speech at the 25th anniversary of that city's Mercantile Library Association. In 1840, the Mormon leader Brigham Young reportedly proclaimed that Illinois would 'become a great and mighty mountain as [a] city set upon a hill that cannot be hid' and prophesied a bright future for Nauvoo as 'the greatest city in the whole world'. And in a controversial speech in Baltimore in 1877, the former slave, abolitionist and black activist Frederick Douglass rebuked a corrupt and degraded Washington, DC, for failing to be a 'city set upon a hill, a source of light, health, and beauty to all who come within its golden radiance'.[25]

None of these alternative uses of Jesus' metaphor achieved the significance later accorded to Winthrop and his discourse when they were turned retrospectively into the origin for the United States as the city on a hill. These other instances form an important, independent stream for the idea of America as the city on a hill, a stream that dried up. Assuming all these documents had been available in print and anthologized in the twentieth century, speechwriters could have quoted from Edwards or another public figure and launched them to prominence in the canon of the American civil religion. John F. Kennedy or Ronald Reagan could have used them – finding in them a far more explicit claim than Winthrop's about America as a city on a hill – but they did not. And those choices made all the difference to the story we remember, to the path we imagine America followed on its way to the city on a hill. The conventional story we tell about the making of this part of the American identity could have been otherwise. There was nothing inevitable about the course it took – not in 1630, or 1738, or 1838.

Now that we have reacquainted ourselves with the 'foreign country' of Puritan New England and witnessed what happened to the metaphor of the city on a hill during the two centuries in which the Model of Christian Charity remained virtually unknown, we are prepared to begin the search in earnest for how America's identity became inseparable from Winthrop's metaphor. So far, we have accounted for the first 200 years of the metaphor's place in American history. In that whole stretch of time, there were no explicit connections yet in the American mind to fuse John Winthrop, his discourse, the city on a hill and the meaning of America. Associations that now appear self-evident to so many Americans and to more than a few foreign observers simply did not exist two centuries ago. The fact that modern commentators turn to the Model of Christian Charity at all to understand the meaning of America is the product of the quirky twists and turns of history.

4

A spectacle to the world, 1838–1930

"But I offer my edifice as a spectacle to the world," said Hollingsworth, "that it may take example and build many another like it. Therefore I mean to set it on the open hill-side."

NATHANIEL HAWTHORNE, *THE BLITHEDALE ROMANCE* (1852)

Nathaniel Hawthorne reached back to New England's Puritan founding and looked forward to America's complex identity as the 'city on a hill' in his 1852 satire, the *Blithedale Romance*. He based his novel loosely on his experience at Brook Farm, the Transcendentalist utopian community founded in West Roxbury, Massachusetts, in 1841. He had already explored the Puritan past in *The Scarlet Letter* (1850) and *The House of the Seven Gables* (1851). That heritage seemed to preoccupy him. His ancestor, William Hawthorne, had arrived in the New World with the first wave of Puritans in 1630. And now he wrestled with the Puritan legacy as it manifested itself in his own generation's reforming zeal. He satirized these modern utopians for casting themselves as the 'descendants of the Pilgrims, whose high enterprise, as we sometimes flattered ourselves, we had taken up, and were carrying it onward and aloft, to a point which they never dreamed of attaining'. For the character of Hollingsworth, the leader of Blithedale, that 'high enterprise' took shape in his imagination as the blueprint for a model community. It would be 'a spectacle to the world', the very words the Reverend William Perkins had used back in Cambridge, England, to explain Matthew 5.14. More than a beacon, though, this 'edifice' would inspire emulators to 'take example and build many another like it'. It would replicate itself and therefore had to be perched 'on the open hill-side' – the very aspiration the egomaniacal Hollingsworth would never attain.

Hawthorne drew attention in 1852 to what we might call the 'dark side' of the professional philanthropist writ large as the Redeemer Nation. The images he chose remind us that some of the questions at stake in a nation's identity as a 'city on a hill' surfaced in American culture in the mid-nineteenth century with or without reference to the exact metaphor. Even though that phrase from the Sermon on the Mount and the Model of Christian Charity had hardly begun to be refashioned from biblical and Puritan metaphor into national myth, the ideas were there in other forms and noticed by the nation's most gifted observers. In some ways, that keen insight makes it all the more remarkable that Hawthorne's generation used Winthrop's discourse and the city on a hill so little to define the American mission. Given the Model of Christian Charity's reputation today, we might expect scholars and politicians to have seized hold of it immediately upon publication in 1838 as a historical discovery of great magnitude and incalculable significance in their quest to understand and mould the American identity. We might naturally fall into imagining that *our* way of reading the document must have been *their* way, for them to have singled out the metaphor of the city on a hill as the highlight of Winthrop's discourse and the interpretive key to American exceptionalism. But they did not. No scholar or statesman left any record of experiencing such an 'aha!' moment when he saw the Model in print. Indeed, it is hard to tell if many people at all noticed the document itself in 1838 let alone the magic words 'city on a hill'. By the 1850s, the unadorned fact that Winthrop wrote a discourse while aboard the *Arbella* started appearing in entries about the governor in biographical dictionaries and encyclopedias. But only in 1858 would excerpts from the Model make their debut in the history books. And that debut was rather timid.

How the document ever came into the hands of the New-York Historical Society in the first place is a bit obscure.[1] From 1630 until 1809, the only known manuscript copy of the Model belonged to the Winthrop family. The records of the Society indicate that on 30 January, Francis B. Winthrop, a direct descendant of the Puritan governor, passed along to the Reverend Samuel Miller a set of 22 rare seventeenth- and eighteenth-century books, sermons, and other manuscripts. The last item on the list describes 'A Modell of Christian Charity written on Board the Ship Arrabella by John Winthrop'.[2] A library catalogue dated 1812 and published the following year acknowledges various donations made by Francis Winthrop and other benefactors but does not yet list the 'Model of Christian Charity' among the Society's extensive holdings.

More than 20 years passed before anyone showed interest in publishing the Model. When the discourse finally made it into print and from there into general circulation and into the history books, it did so in a hurried and carelessly edited version published in Boston by the Massachusetts Historical Society (MHS). Founded in 1791, the Society devoted itself to 'the preservation of books, pamphlets, manuscripts and records' in order to 'rescue the true history of this country from the ravages of time and the effects of ignorance and neglect'. So began the Society's constitution. In explaining itself to the public, the Society offered Winthrop's Journal as an example of just the sort of 'monument' it hoped to preserve. The journal, the public notice continued in elevated style, 'hath been preserved in his family, and hath served as the basis of several histories of New-England'. In 1790, the journal had been published in Hartford by none other than Noah Webster.[3]

The Society quickly fulfilled the promise of its founding.[4] It held meetings, hosted public lectures, amassed documents, published proceedings and collections, built a splendid library and archives, and increased its ranks of resident and corresponding members. Its rolls in the early nineteenth century included John Adams, John Quincy Adams, George Bancroft, Edward Everett, Daniel Webster, Noah Webster and more than half a dozen Winthrops. Its success was soon duplicated by new societies dotting the Eastern seaboard and fledgling organizations reaching into the expanding West. By the late 1830s, the Society's gentlemen historians were more than 20 volumes deep into a project to publish documents of interest to historians and antiquarians.

On the last day of January 1838, the New-York Historical Society's George Folsom (a corresponding member of the Massachusetts Historical Society) wrote to Thaddeus M. Harris – Unitarian minister, distinguished Harvard librarian and the current librarian of the MHS – informing him of a recent motion by his board to copy an unnamed manuscript by John Winthrop 'not in your Library and never published'.[5] Harris wrote back almost immediately to accept the offer and asked Folsom to include 'some prefatory account of the original'.[6] Subsequent correspondence between the two societies showed how eager the MHS was to have the document debut in the next volume of its published collections. By mid-April, Boston had grown impatient with New York, claiming the delay of the Winthrop manuscript was holding up production of the next volume.[7] By mid-May, the document was in hand, a relieved Harris confirmed, and the Model made its debut in August in the *Collections of the Massachusetts Historical Society*, nestled between a Puritan poem entitled 'Our Forefather's Song' and 40 pages of documents on the early history of the post office in Massachusetts.[8]

It is worth trying to imagine what this document sounded like when read for the first time and without a single accretion of later interpretations, quotations, or 'repurposing'. What did these amateur historians and men of letters notice? Only two of them left us much of a clue. James Savage, treasurer of the MHS, added a few 'prefatory remarks' to the Model. As the respected editor of the new edition of Winthrop's Journal published in 1825 that included for the first time the recently discovered third volume, Savage seemed well-equipped to interpret Winthrop's 'homily', as he called it. He numbered Winthrop among those remarkable early settlers whose 'spirit of stern patriotism and equal self denial' built 'the edifice of SUCH an empire, whose whole and true glory was all within their prophetic vision'. He then added the Latin, *Tantum religio potuit* – roughly translated, 'only religion is able to do so much' – either forgetting or not knowing that this was a fragment from Lucretius, the Roman Epicurean poet and philosopher, who completed the line by saying, 'Only religion is able to persuade men to do so much evil'. But Savage had in mind, of course, the great good that Winthrop had done as the embodiment of the virtues of New England's forefathers. His life of service proved 'that he practiced what in this essay is inculcated'.[9]

As requested, Folsom also provided a 'prefatory account' in a letter dated 19 April 1838, and published along with the Model. He mentioned that the transcription was prepared by the assistant librarian – Benjamin Winthrop – but that handwritten copy has not survived in the archives. Folsom wrote, 'I am satisfied, by comparison with the original, that the copy has been accurately made; occasionally, however, a word was illegible, rendering it necessary to leave blanks'. Indeed, the manuscript has pencil marks here and there, including a few question marks in the margins, ghostly traces of where the editors may have struggled to make out troublesome sections. At points, the seventeenth-century handwriting left Folsom baffled, he admitted. He apologized that despite diligent efforts he was 'unable to furnish any additional information relative to the interesting relic of the "brave leader and famous Governor" of the Colony of Massachusetts Bay'. He even seemed uncertain that Francis Winthrop had donated the manuscript.[10]

Comparison with the original and with later editions shows that Benjamin Winthrop's transcription was anything but accurate. He made inconsistent changes to spelling throughout the document, beginning with the title page. He modernized some spellings from the cover but left others in their archaic original. He changed 'Arrabella' to 'Arbella' and 'Attlantick' to 'Atlantic', but kept 'Brittaine' the same. He kept 'soe' but changed 'condicion' to 'condition' and read 'subieccion' as 'submission' instead of 'subjection' and rendered 'World' for 'workes'. He (or the printer) also added italics to biblical quotations according to the convention common in the nineteenth century. These errors and stylistic changes endured for centuries. As the only version prepared from the manuscript for the next 80 years, the document made its way into history books and anthologies in this poor condition. When, for instance, later historians quoted Winthrop's hope that other plantations would ask God to 'make it likely that of New England', they repeated some of the copyist's oddest mistakes. What Folsom and his colleagues clearly did not realize was how famous this document would become . . . eventually.

One magazine did notice the Model almost immediately upon publication. *The American Quarterly Register* served as the mouthpiece of the American Education Society and was published in Boston under various names and editors between 1827 and 1843. In November 1838, the editors spotted in the latest edition of the *Collections* of the Massachusetts Historical Society 'a very interesting article, from which we may make an extract hereafter'. Though a bit tardy, the journal kept its promise two years later by reprinting the entire 'Modell of Christian Charitie', as it called it. The year 1840, therefore, likely marks the moment when Winthrop's discourse reached a general audience for the first time. It would not appear in print again as a complete text until 1917.

But more significant for our purposes than the timing of all this is the note the magazine's editors added and what that comment reveals about how they read the Model and why they decided to reprint it. Their explanation had nothing to do with America's identity as the city on a hill or anything else connected to the meaning of America. Their thoughts travelled in a different direction altogether. The Model, they explained, 'is here inserted for the correct views it contains in respect to charitable contributions, and as being the production of a layman of distinguished talents, piety and standing, and also, as exhibiting the religious character of the Pilgrims of New England'. Upon their first encounter with the document, then, they read it simply as a lay discourse on benevolence and as a window not into the soul of America but into the character of John Winthrop and the religious temperament of their ancestors. Their historical awareness in 1840, even though they mistakenly spoke of the Pilgrims instead of the Puritans, was closer to the truth of Winthrop's intentions than the way modern Americans typically handle him and his discourse. They offered a restrained understanding, free of mythic dimensions. They gave no hint, experienced no premonition, that this document might somehow provide a clue to the American mission. That role for the Model and its metaphor would take more than a century to develop. Even by 1930 that destiny was not yet obvious or assured.

The search for the city on a hill during these years entails piecing together the story of something that did *not* happen, the story of Americans not saying things we think they 'should' have said given the popular version of American history circulating today. And that difficulty brings us back to the point I raised in the Introduction about historians' justified suspicion of arguments based on missing evidence. But in this case, the silence of this 'non-event' has meaning. It points to a significant change over time. We can only recognize the magnitude of the city on a hill as a national symbol today by contrasting it with its former obscurity. We need to encounter the city on a hill first as a 'non-event' in order to understand how people 'repurposed' the metaphor for its current use. This is the story of an absence, but not an absence of something that once was there and then was gone, as if nineteenth-century Americans mislaid it. This was something that was never there to begin with and that no one knew was going to appear later. There was simply no formulaic way yet for them to handle the city on a hill.

In January of 1838, just as the historical societies in Boston and New York began to exchange letters about the Model of Christian Charity, a 28-year-old

Abraham Lincoln addressed the Young Men's Lyceum of Springfield, Illinois. His topic was the 'perpetuation of our political institutions'. An aspiring Whig politician, he drew attention to the pernicious influence of what he called the 'mob' in Jacksonian America and the threat that spirit of lawlessness posed to the edifice of the nation's 'civil and religious liberty'. To counter these forces, he urged his fellow citizens to rededicate themselves to the achievement of the Revolution and the Constitution, cultivating 'reverence for the laws' as the '*political religion* of the nation'.[11]

Lincoln ended his address by wondering how the spirit of the founding era could be kept alive once the last surviving members of that generation died. The nation seemed aware that there was an inexorable movement underway from living history and living memory to the pages of history books. When Ralph Waldo Emerson gave a public oration marking the two-hundredth anniversary of the founding of Concord, Massachusetts, in 1835, a number of elderly veterans of the Battle of Lexington and Concord (1775) had sat before him in the church audience. Perhaps the young Lincoln had witnessed similar celebrations over the past few years in which Revolutionary War veterans had been honoured guests. Whatever the case, he expressed a fear heard often in the first part of the nineteenth century. The physical presence of that generation was quickly ending, and, as their inspiring achievement in 'establishing and maintaining civil and religious liberty' became the stuff of ever more distant and dimmer memory, their animating spirit, their passion for their cause, would inevitably dim as well. 'I do not mean to say', he elaborated, 'that the scenes of the revolution are now or ever will be entirely forgotten; but that like every thing else, they must fade upon the memory of the world, and grow more dim by the lapse of time. In history, we hope, they will be read of, and recounted, so long as the bible shall be read;– but even granting that they will, their influence cannot be what it heretofore has been'. These brave, public-spirited men had been the 'pillars of the temple of liberty'. But now the living generation had to pledge itself to maintain '*general intelligence, sound morality*, and, in particular, *a reverence for the constitution and laws'*. These would comprise the foundation on which 'the proud fabric of freedom [may] rest, as the rock of its basis; and as truly as has been said of the only greater institution, *'the gates of hell shall not prevail against it'*.[12]

The year of Lincoln's speech, 1838, marked the fiftieth anniversary of the ratification of the Constitution, the most recent of a long series of regional and national landmarks that promoted the memory of colonial and Revolutionary America. In 1820, proud New Englanders had observed the two-hundredth anniversary of the Pilgrim landing. The 1820s had also brought around the half-century mark for the Battle of Lexington and Concord, the Declaration of Independence, and Bunker Hill. And 1830 marked the two-hundredth anniversary of Winthrop's arrival. Various 'New England' or 'Pilgrim Societies' were set up by homesick émigrés in New York and even in Charleston, South Carolina, in the early nineteenth century. Daniel Webster, Edward Everett, John Quincy Adams and Justice Joseph Story delivered anniversary orations that drew straight lines from the Puritan colonists to what they considered to be America's principal achievements 200 years later. They narrated New England's history as if it were the history of the whole United States. They made the Puritans the origin (singular) of America and its institutions, character, and mission. New England served as the authentic, normative progenitor of America as a whole, generalizing the rather particular Puritan version of national covenants, holy commonwealths, chosen people and providential nationalism into collective traits of the American people. By mid-century, any other version of the story, or even a diversity of stories, became defined as aberrations or declensions from the model.

The accuracy or justice of the emerging New England narrative in the 1830s is not our primary concern here. The point is that this way of telling the story of America provoked an inter-regional debate that drew in the very historians who soon introduced the Model of Christian Charity into the history books. The modern American historian Harlow Sheidley shows the skill and determination Massachusetts' political and cultural elite brought to their attempt to nationalize their Puritan ancestors into the progenitors of American character and institutions as a whole, the 'seed' of American ideals, and the origin of republicanism, ordered liberty and communal cohesiveness. In this reading, the New England forebears became paragons of order, stability, and self-governance and anything but the nonconformist radicals who had fled England. History became a principal weapon in the sectional politics of the 1830s.[13]

A speech from a New England statesman in 1835 helps make Sheidley's point. Peleg Sprague was invited to give the annual address to the Pilgrim Society of Plymouth.[14] The Massachusetts native and Harvard graduate had made his political career in Maine. He served two terms in the US House and then one term in the Senate before retiring in early 1835. As customary on such occasions, Sprague celebrated the numerical, material and moral progress of New England's 'Puritan Pilgrims', lumping together the colonists of 1620 and 1630 in the way that had become common by the early nineteenth century and helped unify and simplify the story of America's origins. Foremost on his mind, however, were those aspects of the New England character most misunderstood and even 'misrepresented', he charged, not only abroad but also 'by other portions of our own country' – by which he clearly meant the South. He emphasized 'enthusiasm' as the key trait of the Puritan character, and profiled his ancestors as bundles of fiery, restless, impulsive energy kept in check and channeled productively by a collective self-discipline passed down through a 'rigid system of education'.

The fruit of all this Puritan 'zeal' Sprague thought obvious. It was nothing less than the source of American success. 'In every state of the Union', he claimed, 'you will find that they have taken the lead in energy and activity, and wherever there have been the greatest advances, there you will be sure to find the sons of New England. The Puritan blood flows everywhere, swelling every vein of the great republic, diluted perhaps by intermixture, enfeebled perhaps, but still imparting something of its pristine strength and ardor'. Further on in his remarks, Sprague cast Massachusetts as the sole impetus behind the Revolutionary War. New England, and Massachusetts in particular, stood among the states as the 'first in magnanimity, foremost in dangers, freest in her blood and treasures, ever impelled onwards by a deep, pervading, original enthusiasm'.

Some might, and did, prefer to call that enthusiasm fanaticism. But the point was that New England in the 1830s promoted itself in this and similar ways as the key to the American narrative. One Virginian writing for the *Southern Literary Messenger*, who read parts of Sprague's address in an 1837 article in the *North American Review* on the question of New England's reputation, seized this opportunity to emphasize the different origins of the North and the South. Massachusetts might well boast of its Puritan origins, but that was precisely the problem as far as this Virginian was concerned: 'We, too, of the south, and especially of Virginia, are the descendants, for the most part, of the old cavaliers – the enemies and persecutors of those old puritans – and entertain, perhaps, unwittingly, something of an hereditary and historical antipathy against the children, for their fathers' sake'.[15]

Whatever else this exchange pointed to in the sectional 'culture wars' heating up in the 1830s, it shows the problem of trying to force the history of a diverse, federated republic into a single story. Southerners resented being absorbed into the story of Plymouth Rock as much as New Englanders would have resented being informed that the 'blood' of Cavaliers 'flows everywhere', at least in the veins of New England's finest leaders and where it has not been 'diluted'. This point had been made more clearly about two years earlier in the *Southern Literary Messenger* in a review of the first volume of a new history of the United States. The anonymous reviewer found himself repeatedly 'disappointed', despite the New England author's obvious intention to praise the reviewer's Virginia ancestors. That praise masked a 'more mischievous' design, he suspected. The historian tried to remake colonial Virginians into supporters of Parliament and Cromwell during the English Civil Wars of the 1640s, and not loyal subjects to the crown, thereby transforming them into ideological descendants of the Puritan revolutionaries and forcing them into a tidy, single American story at the expense of what made a state like Virginia its own kind of place and not just another version of New England. To be sure, the larger political conflict of the 1830s over the nature of the Union was involved here, but the reviewer's point was more precise than simply another volley in that sectional battle. 'Whether for better or worse', he wrote, '[Virginia] differs essentially from that of every other people under the sun. How long it shall be before the "*march of mind*", as it is called, in its Juggernaut car, shall pass over us, and crush and obliterate every trace of what our ancestors were, and what we ourselves have been, is hard to say. It may postpone that evil day, to resist any attempt to impress us with false notions of our early history, and the character of our ancestors'. 'Let them write our books and they become our masters', he warned.[16]

The author who provoked this Virginian was the young historian George Bancroft.[17] At the time, the former schoolmaster was just beginning to make his mark as a man of letters. Today, he is nearly forgotten, but by the end of his long career as a scholar and public servant he would stand as one of the most famous authors in America. The first volume of his never-completed *History of the United States* appeared in 1834, the start of what would become the single bestselling history of America published in the nineteenth century. One of Bancroft's biographers estimates that one in three households in New England eventually owned a set of Bancroft. And his books found an audience even in the South despite the occasional hostile review defending regional particularity.

Bancroft graduated from Harvard in 1817 with a degree in divinity. He seemed destined to follow his father into a career as a Unitarian minister. But with the encouragement and financial help of Harvard's president and a small circle of benefactors, he pursued a doctorate in philosophy at the University of Göttingen and further study at Berlin, becoming one of the first Americans to earn a Ph.D. Upon returning to the United States, he founded a prestigious boys' school near Northampton, Massachusetts, site of Edwards' revivals a century before. He became active in Massachusetts politics as a Jacksonian Democrat in the 1830s as he worked on the first installments of his *History*. His correspondents included Martin Van Buren, James Buchanan, John C. Calhoun, Edward Everett, Stephen Douglas, Ralph Waldo Emerson, Theodore Parker, Julia Ward Howe, Henry Wadsworth Longfellow, Orestes Brownson, Washington Irving and other leading statesmen and authors. His remarkable political career from the 1840s to the 1870s included appointments as Secretary of the Navy, foreign minister to Britain, and finally minister to Prussia and the newly formed German Empire. In fits and starts over these decades, his ever-expanding *History* grew to ten ponderous volumes and went through multiple new editions.

Bancroft's files, preserved in dozens of mostly uncatalogued boxes in the Manuscript Division of the New York Public Library, reveal a lot about his habits as a researcher, writer and reviser. He was an obsessive tinkerer who left nothing untouched. Multiple personal copies of each volume of the *History* have survived – dusty, fragile, tied with string, annotated and sometimes bulging with interleaved notes and clippings. He corrected errors, fussed with nuances of wording and punctuation, and amended his footnotes (before eventually dispensing with them altogether). Two of the archival boxes in New York contain copies of Volume I, including two bound volumes specially made for him by the publisher with blank pages ready for annotations inserted between every page of printed text.

Not all the ideas in his marginal notes for new or altered material made it into new editions, of course. And only two changes out of potentially thousands relate directly to the search for America's identity as the city on a hill. The inventory of Bancroft's personal library shows that he owned a copy of the 1838 *Collections* in which Winthrop's Model appeared. Despite several opportunities to add the discourse on charity to his account of Winthrop and the Puritan colony, he waited 20 years to do anything with the document. Not until the extensively revised sixteenth edition, published in June of 1858, did the Model of Christian Charity make its debut in Bancroft's *History*. Indeed, this new edition may have been the first time any historian quoted from the Model and the first time since the 1600s that the words 'city on a hill' were used directly to define the Puritan project.

But the way Bancroft chose to hitch the 'city on a hill' to the Puritans is not what a modern reader expects. His use of the metaphor in 1858 seems straightforward enough at first glance: '[The Puritans] desired to be bound together in a most intimate and equal intercourse, for one and the same great end. They knew that they would be as a city set upon a hill, and that the eyes of all people were upon them'.[18] The curious thing here is that Bancroft thought it unnecessary to mention either Winthrop or the Model of Christian Charity. In fact, he did not indicate that the phrase was a quotation from anywhere at all. It is highly unlikely that a general reader in 1858 would have recognized these words as anything other than an allusion to Matthew 5.14. That reader would not have 'heard' John Winthrop when he saw the phrases 'city set upon a hill' or 'eyes of all people'.

That this is the case becomes obvious in the next of the paragraphs Bancroft reworked for the new edition. He added a long quotation from an unnamed document – though he skipped some words, changed others, and left out long passages without bothering with ellipses – a surprisingly common practice among historians in the nineteenth century and a technique Bancroft was never shy about. This is the whole paragraph he added:

"The worke we have in hand" – these are Winthrop's words on board the Arbella during the passage – "is by a mutuall consent, through a speciall overruling Providence, and a more than ordinary approbation of the church of Christ, to seek out a place of cohabitation and consortshipp under a due forme of government, both civill and ecclesiastical. For this wee are entered into covenant with God; for this wee must be knit together as one man, always having before our eyes our commission as members of the same body. Soe shall wee keepe the unitie of the spirit in the bond of peace. The Lord will be our God, and delight to dwell among us, as his owne people; we shall see much more of his wisdome, power, goodness, and truthe, than formerly wee have been acquainted with; Hee shall make us a prayse and glory, that men shall say of succeeding plantations, 'the Lord make it likely that of New England'".

This passage comes, of course, from the Model of Christian Charity as published in 1838 and retains its spellings and transcription errors. I say 'of course', but there was nothing obvious about this source for a reader in 1858. Bancroft attributed the words to Winthrop, but that is all he bothered to mention. At no point did Bancroft give the Model of Christian Charity by name as the source of these largely unfamiliar words. He had even dispensed with footnotes by this point in his new editions, so the reader was left without a clue as to the origin of Winthrop's shipboard advice.

One obvious conclusion, then, is that the Model of Christian Charity had not yet been accorded its canonical status in antebellum America. Bancroft left Winthrop's discourse unidentified and invisible to his readers. And his readers would not have known what they were missing. Nor would they have been likely to know that the next words in this quotation from Winthrop's unidentified document were none other than 'For wee must consider that wee shall be as a citty upon a hill. The eies of all people are upon us'. The very phrases no historian, political theorist, politician or pundit in the twenty-first century could imagine leaving out were entirely optional to Bancroft in 1858. Right through the last edition in 1883, America's pre-eminent historian left this new section unchanged and never explicitly connected the 'city on a hill' to John Winthrop or the Model of Christian Charity.

None of this is to suggest that Bancroft did not promote the idea of an exemplary America called to be a light to the world. Bancroft called the Puritans who settled in Salem in 1629, just ahead of the more famous migration led by Winthrop, 'the depositories of the purest truth, and the selected instruments to kindle in the wilderness the beacon of pure religion, of which the undying light should not only penetrate the wigwams of the heathen, but spread its benignant beams across the darkness of the whole civilized world'.[19] And in an 1854 lecture to the New-York Historical Society he said, 'Our country is bound to allure the world to freedom by the beauty of its example'. It was this sort of airy idealism that prompted Orestes Brownson to complain in a scathing review of Volume IV of the *History* in 1852 that his onetime friend wrote metaphysics and theology masquerading as history and did so with the 'zeal of the missionary'. 'Mr. Bancroft', he mocked, 'finds that the original purpose of creation, of God and the universe, is fulfilled in the establishment of American democracy'.[20] That kind of teleology was the sort of thing that had disturbed the reviewer for the *Southern Literary Messenger* back in 1835. And in 1838, the Scottish historian Thomas Carlyle felt it necessary to remind his 'didactic' colleague that 'all things have light *and* shadow'.[21] The point is that Bancroft developed his mythic America without Winthrop's Model, ignored it for decades after it appeared, and then used it to confirm what he already believed about the Puritans and their role in the inexorable march of human liberty. The Model simply took its assigned place in a system Bancroft had already constructed.

The number of times the Model was quoted and anthologized multiplied rapidly after mid-century, though historians and politicians still felt free to ignore it. Just months after Bancroft's revised edition appeared in 1858, the former Unitarian minister, Harvard Divinity School dean, and antislavery 'conscience' Whig politician John Gorham Palfrey published Volume I of his *History of New England*. A later historian said of Palfrey that in his life's work 'this leading representative of the filiopietistic school of historians set up an impermanent monument as a token of his ancestor worship'.[22] Regarding the Model, Palfrey simply noted, 'On the voyage Winthrop composed a little treatise, which he called "A Model of Christian Charity".' The description that Palfrey added was short and unadorned: 'It breathes the noblest spirit of philanthropy. The reader's mind kindles as it enters into the train of thought in which the author referred to "the work we have in hand". "It is," he said, "by mutual consent, through a special overruling Providence, and a more than ordinary approbation of the churches of Christ, to seek out a place of cohabitation and consortship *under a due form of government both civil and ecclesiastical*". The forms and institutions under which liberty, civil and religious, is consolidated and assured, were floating vaguely in the musings of that hour'.[23] Palfrey's eye went to the same closing section of the Model that had attracted Bancroft, but he, too, stopped short of the 'city on a hill' and never quoted it. He accepted the fact that the Model was written during the voyage, drew attention to the Puritan colonists' 'work', and read this language as a mark of the settlers' spirit of 'philanthropy' – a reading close to the one offered by the editors of *The American Quarterly Register* back in 1840. Beyond that, Palfrey saw Winthrop's aspirations as somehow foreshadowing religious and civil liberty. But still no 'city on a hill'.

Not finding the city on a hill mentioned in a context like this is the sort of oddity that provoked the questions in my mind that eventually led to this book. As I noted in the Introduction, a few years ago I happened to be reading the 'Historical Introduction' to John Wingate Thornton's *The Pulpit of the American Revolution*, published in 1860.[24] The Harvard-trained lawyer and antiquarian surveyed the religious impulse behind the Puritan settlement of New England. In so doing, he tried to establish a precedent for the kind of political sermons popular during the Revolution and to trace American independence directly back to the 'Puritan pulpit'. What struck me at the time was that he never mentioned Winthrop's Model of Christian Charity or the city on a hill. And this just weeks after Lincoln's election and when the Union and America's future were at stake. This became the first 'dog that didn't bark'. Since then, I have learned that throughout the nineteenth century all sorts of people talked about Winthrop without the Model and the metaphor (as Thornton felt free to do) and used the metaphor without Winthrop and the Model. Thornton's neglect of the Model turns out to have been typical of his generation.

During the Civil War, the metaphor of the city on a hill appeared both North and South and apart from any association with Winthrop or the Model. The South's use of the metaphor might come as a surprise given the region's reaction to Bancroft, but in the few instances I am aware of no Southerner attached the metaphor to the Puritans. Nevertheless, the impulse to connect the fracturing United States and then the Confederacy with the biblical city on a hill was very much present below the Mason-Dixon Line. On 21 November 1860, a 'day of fasting, humiliation and prayer' proclaimed by the South Carolina legislature and the very day John Wingate Thornton finished writing his preface up in Boston, the eminent Presbyterian minister James Henley Thornwell preached a 'Sermon on National Sins'.[25] As a pastor, president of South Carolina College until 1855, and then professor at Columbia Theological Seminary, the Old School divine had staunchly defended the 'spirituality of the church', that is, a strict separation of the church from politics. He began his fast-day sermon by reinforcing this doctrine and practice: 'I have no design . . . to intimate that there is a parallel between Jerusalem and our own Commonwealth in relation to the Covenant of God'. He defended his practice over the years of keeping politics out of the pulpit, and seemed more than a bit self-conscious about now preaching on the fate of the Union. He lamented the impending 'ruin of a great nation'. America had not survived a century since its founding. Its institutions, once 'the hope and admiration of the world', plunged toward destruction in the wake of Lincoln's election. And 'the fraud which makes our government a failure', he warned, 'must darken the prospects of liberty throughout the world'.

Most striking in Thornwell's sermon is his simultaneous embrace of America's intended role in the world and lament over the loss of that destiny. His use of the past tense is telling: 'It was ours to redeem this continent, to spread freedom, civilization and religion through the whole length of the land. Geographically placed between Europe and Asia, we were, in some sense, the representatives of the human race. The fortunes of the world were in our hand'. And then he appropriated Matthew 5.14 in a way that would seem to have contradicted his theology of the spirituality of the church: 'We were a city set upon a hill, whose light was intended to shine upon every people and upon every land. To forego this destiny, to forfeit this inheritance, and that through bad faith, is an enormity of treason equaled only by the treachery of a Judas, who betrayed his Master with a kiss'. Thornwell's searing accusation against the North and its bad faith toward the Constitution never questioned America's high calling in history as an earthly city on a hill. Indeed, it presupposed it.

In bidding farewell to a failed union, Thornwell may have articulated the most direct reference yet in American history to the United States as a city on a hill. To be sure, the Columbia pastor did not speak for the South as a whole or even for South Carolina. And there is no reason to think that by invoking the city on a hill he meant to root America in New England. He used the metaphor independently of Winthrop, the Model, and Puritanism. There is the intriguing possibility, however, that the Presbyterian minister picked up the language of America as the 'city on a hill' from none other than the vaguely pantheistic George Bancroft. Bancroft heard Thornwell preach in Columbia in 1855 while on a research trip through South Carolina and got to know him and his family. The following year, Thornwell asked Bancroft to write for the *Southern Quarterly Review*, over which he had just assumed the editorship, and to put him in contact with other New York and Boston writers.[26] He also visited Bancroft in New York in 1856 while on church business. About this time, Bancroft was working on revisions to Volume I of his *History*, but we can only speculate about any direct influence he may have had on Thornwell.

During the war itself, other Southern pastors identified the Confederacy as a 'city on a hill'. A tract attributed to Methodist minister Herbert T. Bacon, and optimistically entitled 'Our Triumph', opened with an appeal to Southern soldiers: 'Brethren of the Confederate Army:–I humbly hope and pray that at no very distant day, a triumph glorious and decisive awaits our cause, that gentle peace with all its attendant blessings will smile upon our land, and the lovely sisters liberty and independence will take up their abodes in our midst; then our agony of strife and glory passed, our country purified by her trials and sufferings, made wiser, better and holier by her chastisements, will start afresh in her career, and "like a city set upon a hill," fulfill her God-given mission to exalt in civilization and christianity [sic] the nations of the earth'.[27]

Such a sense of mission was not unique to these Southerners, of course. More elaborately, the Reverend Stephen Alexander Hodgman described the American mission and destiny in *The Great Republic Judged, But Not Destroyed*. Near the end of his popular book, the idealistic Union army chaplain asked:

Who can doubt, that, when this war is over we shall be a greater and a more liberty-loving people than ever before? Our mission is to give to the nations of the earth, a practical demonstration of the great problem, never before solved, that, *man is capable of self government*. It is to be our destiny, to teach all tyrants and oppressors, that their days are numbered. We are to be a city set on a hill, whose light cannot be hid. With what fond anticipations, and earnest, kindling hopes, the eyes of millions, are, at this moment, turned toward this land![28]

For all three ministers, the metaphor of the city on a hill served as a vehicle for Christian republicanism, imperiled, righteous and restored. It stood for a nation purified by war and restored to its place as an example to the world and, for Hodgman, a warning to tyrants. It described what America had failed to be, what the Confederacy was called to be, and what the Union had finally vindicated. But however widespread the use of the metaphor may have been during the war (and it does not appear to have been very great), such use does not seem to have affected the way people interpreted John Winthrop or read and quoted from the Model of Christian Charity. The phrase 'city on a hill' still did not leap from the pages of Winthrop's discourse after the war. There is no indication that the trauma of the Civil War divided the story of America as the city on a hill into pre- and post-war phases.

John Winthrop's standing among America's founding fathers, an honour he had enjoyed since at least 1702 when Cotton Mather extolled him as the American Nehemiah, seemed to become only more secure after the Union victory. In the 1860s and 1870s, the State of Massachusetts and the Winthrop family took care to preserve and perpetuate Winthrop's legacy. Near the end of the war, the United States Congress invited each state to send one or two statues to adorn the old House chamber, rechristened 'National Statuary Hall' in 1864. In 1865 the governor of Massachusetts duly appointed a committee (historian John Palfrey among them). The members easily agreed to recommend John Winthrop but divided over whether the other statue should be of John Adams or his cousin Sam. A final decision was delayed until the legislature acted in 1872 by choosing Sam Adams but then dividing over whether Winthrop or a Plymouth leader should represent the colonial epoch. The deadlocked legislature directed a new commission to arrange for a statue of Sam Adams and to pick another from a list of popular early settlers. They chose Winthrop. The $10,000 Italian marble statue was finally set up in the nation's capital in 1876, the year of the American centennial.[29]

About the same time, the Winthrop family made the first of a century of benefactions to the parish church of St. Bartholomew's in Groton, Suffolk – the church where John Winthrop had been baptized into the Church of England in 1588 and at the time of writing a designated stop on the 'American Heritage Trail'. The family returned the brass plaque from Adam Winthrop's grave that had somehow ended up in its possession in America. Continuing down until at least the 1980s, the Winthrops helped repair the church's roof, pipe organ, west tower and porch, and stained glass windows. The large east window over the altar bears most directly on the search for the city on a hill. Donated in 1875, it depicts one scene from the Old Testament and one from the New. On the left, Moses bids farewell to the children of Israel before they enter the Promised Land without him. The biblical reference given underneath is Deuteronomy 30.16, the very words Winthrop had adapted to close his Model: 'I call heaven and earth to record this day against you, that I have set before you life and death, blessing and cursing: therefore choose life, that both thou and thy seed may live'. On the right, the Apostle Paul stands before the elders of the Ephesian church to give his own tearful farewell as recorded in Acts 20.17–38. The implied third image, of course, was Winthrop's farewell to Old England led by God's call. The top of the window gives five of the Beatitudes from the Sermon on the Mount.

Aside from being memorialized in Italian marble and stained glass, Winthrop was also honoured in print by his most eminent descendant, the former Whig Speaker of the House of Representatives, Robert C. Winthrop. Winthrop had entered state politics in 1834 as a fierce opponent of Andrew Jackson. In the US House, he served as a conservative, pro-industrial Whig who opposed the annexation of Texas and the expansion of slavery, but preferred compromise with the South to the destruction of the Union and took a more moderate stance than 'conscience' Whigs like Palfrey. He left public office after 1850 when he failed to hold onto Daniel Webster's vacated Senate seat. In 1860, he supported the Constitutional Union party over Lincoln, and in 1864 backed Lincoln's Democratic challenger, George McClellan. He devoted the rest of his long life to a number of causes, including the Boston Public Library, the Massachusetts Historical Society (which he served as president for nearly 30 years), and preserving the memory of his ancestor John Winthrop.

To that end, he produced a two-volume *Life and Letters of John Winthrop* (1864 and 1867). Collections of this sort were common in the nineteenth century as a way to honour the memory of a distinguished public figure by combining, as the title suggests, excerpts from documents with narrative commentary. The second volume included a long extract from the 1838 edition of the Model of Christian Charity, the longest to date.[30] He modernized most spellings, changed or rearranged a few words and introduced new errors. Into the twentieth century, these paragraphs served as one of the most common sources for scholars working with the discourse. Volume II picked up the story of the Puritan refugees in 1630, just as the fleet prepared to leave the Isle of Wight and the Governor began keeping his journal. Following the sequence of the journal entries closely, Robert Winthrop paused after Sunday, May 2, to introduce the Model of Christian Charity: 'It would seem, however, that Mr. Phillips may not have been the only preacher on board the Arbella during this memorable voyage'. He then gave the long, full title from the discourse's cover page and offered a bit of analysis before moving on to the excerpt. He noted:

In this discourse, after an elaborate discussion of Christian charity or love, the Governor proceeded to speak of the great work in which they had embarked, and of the means by which it was to be accomplished. The spirit of the whole is condensed in the following passage from the conclusion:–
"Thus stands the case between God and us. We are entered into a Covenant with Him for this work. We have taken out a commission. . . .".

From this point, the quotation continued in full all the way through the discourse's final reworking of Moses's farewell. He needed more than 60 lines of text to find the document's 'spirit'. He acknowledged that Winthrop never referred to the discourse in his journal but, wanting the Model to be more than the private musings of a man filling the hours on a long ocean voyage, he speculated that 'the author of it . . . found some fit occasion for delivering what he had taken such pains to write'. It is interesting in light of later confusion and error to see that Robert Winthrop knew that there was no surviving evidence that his ancestor had delivered the Model.

Beyond the *Life and Letters*, the Model of Christian Charity gradually became incorporated into what is often called the 'canon' of American literature. Today, Winthrop's Model can be found among other Puritan authors in almost any anthology of American literature, such as the bestselling *Norton Anthology of American Literature*, a standard survey textbook used at countless colleges and universities. It was accorded that place slowly in the late nineteenth century.[31] The interpretation of the document as part of the nation's literature began in earnest in 1878 when the noted University of Michigan English professor, Moses Coit Tyler, discussed the Model of Christian Charity in the first installment of his multi-volume study of American literature.[32] The Connecticut-born, Yale-educated scholar focused on the discourse's last paragraph, part of the section that Robert Winthrop a decade before had thought 'condensed' the spirit of the Model so admirably. Delving into Winthrop's mind as he pondered the most urgent needs of the Puritan community, Tyler drew attention to what he called its 'Christ-like spirit of disinterestedness'. Only by practicing such self-sacrifice, he wrote, could the colony escape 'becoming base, discordant, and disappointing'. He called the Model 'an elaborate exposition of the Christian doctrine of unselfishness'. At its heart lay what a later generation would call 'communitarian' values. At this point, Tyler quoted Winthrop's admonition to his fellow settlers to 'be knit together in this work as one man'.

Historians continued to quote or ignore the Model as it suited their purposes. Washington University professor John Fiske, who tried to read history through the lens of the evolutionary theories of Charles Darwin and Herbert Spencer, managed to call Winthrop the 'Moses' of the 'Puritan exodus'. In doing so, he drew a parallel common in the seventeenth century and implied most recently in the stained glass window at Groton. But Fisk never cited the Model of Christian Charity.[33] Back in Boston, the former Unitarian minister and Harvard Divinity School professor George E. Ellis, who followed Robert Winthrop as president of the Massachusetts Historical Society, quoted from the Model in his history of seventeenth-century Massachusetts because he believed that he found in its pages what he called Winthrop's 'master motive'. In short, '[Winthrop] believed that his Company had entered on a covenant with each other which was at the same time a Covenant with God: constancy and fidelity exhibited in mutual love were the terms pledged. The enterprise demanded resolution of spirit, for it was hazardous, and might end in disaster; but he would abide by it. He never looked backward; he never saw his native land again'.[34]

Writing at the same time as Fiske and Ellis, Oxford University historian John Andrew Doyle called the Model 'a short and clear statement of the principles on which Christian men should live together'. Chief among those principles, Doyle argued, was the moral framework necessary for private property to be reconciled with the needs of the community. Use of property must be guided by 'the free spirit of Christian charity and brotherly love'. And then Doyle drew attention to the exemplary nature of the Puritan project. 'Selfishness' would bring shame on this work of God. But 'if they should succeed, then men would say of other plantations in later days, "The Lord make it like that of New England"'.[35]

A more surprising and revealing handling of the Model of Christian Charity appeared in the 1891 Winthrop biography I mentioned in the Introduction. The colourful Joseph Hopkins Twichell happened to be Mark Twain's closest friend and travelling companion. An old-stock Puritan and abolitionist, he was educated at Yale and then at Union Theological Seminary and Andover. He served as a Union army chaplain with a New York regiment until 1864 before taking up his calling as a Congregationalist minister in Hartford and as an amateur historian. About a quarter of the way into his biography, when Twichell came to Winthrop's 'elaborate discourse', he quoted the same closing section that attracted his contemporaries: 'The Lord will be our God, and . .

. make us a praise and a glory, that men shall say of succeeding plantations, "The Lord make it likely that of New England". 'Not often in the course of human experience', he added immediately, 'has plainer living gone with higher thinking than on board the Arbella in 1630'.[36]

In 1904, Columbia University historian Herbert Levi Osgood emphasized the uniqueness of Puritan motivations in the age of European colonization. They did not set out for New England to seek personal fortune or to extend the English empire. Instead, religious purposes drew them on. They intended to set up, in Winthrop's words, 'a due form of government both civil and ecclesiastical'. And Osgood, like other historians of the time, emphasized the communal aspects of Winthrop's thought. For this enterprise to flourish, the public had to take precedence over the private. To prove this, he then quoted from the closing paragraphs of the discourse.[37]

Twenty years later, the influential Progressive historian Vernon L. Parrington surveyed Winthrop in his Pulitzer Prize-winning *Main Currents in American Thought*. The University of Washington professor of English acknowledged that his 'point of view' as a scholar was 'liberal rather than conservative, Jeffersonian rather than Federalistic'. His intention for this project, he wrote, was 'to give some account of the genesis and development of certain germinal ideas that have come to be reckoned traditionally American . . .'. He was most interested in what happened to transplanted European ideas once they became 'domesticated' in American soil. Coming to the Puritans, he grouped the 'magistrate' Winthrop alongside the 'priest' John Cotton as the two 'Chief Stewards of Theocracy'.[38] He was not a fan. Indeed, though not as harsh as some of the notorious 'debunkers' of the Puritan legacy in the 1920s, he worked to undermine the notion that America's finest institutions came via the Puritans. Winthrop, far from being a source of democracy, was for Parrington an authoritarian theocrat who tried to perpetuate the old aristocratic order and thwart democracy and popular sovereignty at every turn. Nevertheless, he praised the governor for exhibiting occasional glimmers of the ethic of 'stewardship' that checked some of the worst tendencies of theocratic absolutism embodied in the ideal of the 'elder-magistrate'. 'This nobler spirit of Calvinistic stewardship', Parrington wrote, 'is revealed in Winthrop's *Modell of Christian Charity*, written on shipboard during the voyage out. A sense of profound responsibility devolving upon the leaders imparts dignity to the thought: they must bear and forbear, knitting themselves together in a common purpose, and seeing that "the care of the public" should "oversway all private interests". And this "care of the public", remained in theory if not always in practice, the guiding principle of Winthrop's official activities'.[39]

From the 1860s through the 1920s, from Robert Winthrop through V. L. Parrington, from orators to historians, biographers and literature professors, the Model of Christian Charity was gradually made into a more and more familiar part of the story of Winthrop and the Puritans. Scholars found evidence in the Model for the centrality of Christian love to the 'work' of founding the Puritan colony, for an admirable spirit of 'disinterestedness' and 'unselfishness', for the idea of the covenant in civil society, for communal bonds of brotherhood, and for the ideal of stewardship embodied in the godly magistrate. Some emphasized its religious principles, others its more earthly aspirations for a well-ordered commonwealth. But they handled the Model in a way that Winthrop himself would have recognized as at least approaching his meaning. Whatever the varying shades of interpretation and differences in emphasis, there was one thing all of these authors had in common: not one of them mentioned the 'city on a hill'. They made no connection between the biblical metaphor and the American identity, no connection between the hilltop city and America's mission, exceptionalism, or messianic consciousness. If there was ever a case of something being 'conspicuous by its absence', this was it.

True, Robert Winthrop had included the words 'city on a hill' in his long excerpt in the *Life and Letters*. But that is all he did. He did not single them out or draw attention to them as having special significance. He offered no meditation on their meaning, no hint that somehow they prefigured America's future greatness, nothing to suggest that these were words of prophecy. The former Speaker of the House credited his ancestor with 'laying broad and deep the foundations of an independent republic', but to the metaphor of the city he assigned no importance. He had used the metaphor in the 1840s to describe Boston and he would do so again in the 1880s, but here in 1867 he left the 'city on a hill' embedded in its context. Significantly, the reviewer of Volume II of the *Life and Letters* for the *North American Review* took no notice of the Model or the city on a hill either, the very things a modern reviewer would race to as of the highest importance. He even entertained the heresy that this companion volume was less interesting than the first one 'because the new material brought forward is less striking and characteristic than that which was contained in his first volume, and because there was not much more to be learned about Governor Winthrop's life in New England'.[40] Who today could imagine the Model of Christian Charity having once seemed 'less striking and characteristic' than Winthrop's other works?

One thing these offhanded comments demonstrate is that the Model's pride of place in the American Scripture is retrospective. Winthrop's discourse began appearing in books in a way that had little to do with its later status. I have not found a single historian before 1930, and really not before the 1950s, who extracted the words 'city on a hill' from Winthrop's discourse as the key to the American mission. As scholars prior to 1930 grappled with the significance of the Puritan colonization of New England, they did not know they were supposed to handle the Model of Christian Charity according to a script. That script had not yet been written. They did not repeat an orthodox gloss on the discourse. They did not recite the 'city on a hill' as a creedal affirmation of faith. Before 1858, it was entirely possible to interpret Winthrop's place in American history without recourse to the Model or the metaphor. By 1930, though the Model had become an object of interest in the landscape of early American history, it was still possible and commonplace to interpret the Model without the city on a hill – a striking omission given the metaphor's later history and the false memory that its celebrity status created in the American mind.

5

The revolutionary city, 1930–1969

We in this country, in this generation, are – by destiny rather than choice – the watchmen on the walls of world freedom.

JOHN F. KENNEDY, 1963

On 6 June 1930 – 300 years to the day since the *Arbella* passengers first spotted the coasts of Nova Scotia and Maine – the Boston-based *Christian Science Monitor* ran the latest in a series of imaginative 'daily dispatches' about the Puritans' voyage. Frank Bridgman, clerk of the Massachusetts House of Representatives, prepared these brief articles, writing as if he were a shipboard correspondent in 1630. The *Monitor* vouched for the historical accuracy of every detail, but Bridgman managed to embellish the story just a bit. He imagined hearing on that Lord's Day 'a carefully prepared discourse by Governor Winthrop' who had been asked by the Reverend Phillips to 'take one of today's services' to explain the purpose of their venture. 'For this end, we must be knit together in this work as one man', Bridgman reported, quoting from the Model of Christian Charity. He ended with the inspiring hope 'that men shall say of succeeding plantations, The Lord make it like that of New England'. Typical of the time, he stopped just short of the 'city upon a hill'.

The tercentenary of the Puritan landing provided an occasion not just for creative journalists to reach back to that event but also for historians to reconsider the origins of Massachusetts Bay and the colony's significance to the nation. Among these scholars was the towering figure of Samuel Eliot Morison. Born in Boston in 1887 and reared among the patricians of Beacon Hill, Morison completed his undergraduate and graduate degrees across the Charles River at Harvard. After teaching for a short time at the University of California, Berkeley, he returned to Harvard where he taught for 40 years until his retirement in 1955. From 1922 to 1925 he held the first appointment as Harmsworth Professor of American History at Oxford University (1922–1925) and wrote the two-volume *Oxford History of the United States* (1927), later adapted for American students as *The Growth of the American Republic*, a standard textbook for many years. In 1928, he joined with his Harvard colleagues Kenneth Murdoch and Perry Miller to found the *New England Quarterly*. A man of boundless energy and an ethic of public service, he took time away from his academic career to serve in both the First and Second World Wars. President Franklin Roosevelt, a Harvard classmate and friend, appointed him to serve with the Navy in 1941 in order to write an insider's history of that branch's wartime operations, a work he completed in 15 volumes in 1962. An avid sailor, his biographies of Christopher Columbus and John Paul Jones won the Pulitzer Prize in 1943 and 1959, respectively.

In 1917, the year the United States entered the First World War, the 30-year-old Morison brought out the first new edition of the Model of Christian Charity since 1838. Working from the manuscript in New York, he prepared the most accurate version to date.[1] It comes as no surprise, then, that he quoted from the Model in 1930 for his sketch of John Winthrop in his *Builders of the Bay Colony*, a biographical study of about a dozen Puritan leaders during the colony's first half-century.[2] Morison was a Democrat and Wilsonian idealist who found the cynical 'debunkers' of the 1920s irksome. Not all Ivy Leaguers had awoken after the Great War like F. Scott's Fitzgerald's

Amory Blaine to find 'all Gods dead, all wars fought, all faiths in man shaken'.[3] Nevertheless, his avowed intention in this book was to open up some distance between these adventurous spirits and modern political, social and economic ideology. 'Their object', he wrote of the settlers, 'was not to establish prosperity or prohibition, liberty or democracy, or indeed anything of currently recognized value'. 'My attitude toward seventeenth-century puritanism', he admitted, 'has passed through scorn and boredom to a warm interest and respect. The ways of the puritans are not my ways, and their faith is not my faith; nevertheless they appear to me a courageous, humane, brave, and significant people'.[4]

Coming to Winthrop's 'sermon', as he called it, he drew attention to the similarities between the shipboard discourse and John Cotton's Southampton sermon but found Winthrop's words to embody a more compelling expression of the key to the Puritan community's future. That essential trait was nothing other than brotherly love. For the experiment to succeed, the public interest had to be paramount over private ambition. Morison then claimed, quoting a large part of the Model's conclusion, including the phrase 'city upon a hill': 'Herein is the clearest statement we have of the principles that guided the leaders of the Bay Colony, and their conception of the sort of commonwealth they were to found. It explains much that followed, both good and bad, in the early history of Massachusetts. We need not expect men who believe that they have a commission directly from God, to be eager to share their responsibility or power with others. We should not look to them to be tolerant of other points of view, to suffer the foxes to spoil the vines which they have tenderly planted. The rights of the individual they will hold as nothing in the scales against the public interest, as they conceive it. King Charles I, too, believed in his divine commission. John Winthrop will serve his people according to his lights, and serve them well; but he will make some of the same mistakes as those of his sovereign'.[5]

While not sympathetic with the 'debunkers', Morison clearly took care not to make the New England Puritans into progenitors of democracy, tolerance and individual rights. This same caution was evident in the work of other scholars in 1930. Two essays appeared that year in Morison's *New England Quarterly*, one on Winthrop's political philosophy and the other on his economic views. They concluded that the Bay Colony's governor shared more in common with medieval Europe than with Herbert Hoover's America.[6] In his politics, Winthrop was aristocratic, monarchical and anti-democratic. In his economics, he retained such notions as the just-price theory and other elements of medieval Christendom. In short, Winthrop's thought was anything but a prototype of the United States' civil and religious liberty, and free-market economics. Perhaps the more communitarian Winthrop would appeal to a nation plunged into a deep and worsening economic depression. To be sure, an ostensibly more historically accurate Winthrop might prove useful for liberals eager to find a precedent for Washington DC to take more direct, collective action. Then as now, the search for a 'usable past' knows no ideological boundaries.

Whatever the case, by 1930 Morison had made little use of the city on a hill and handled it in a way that his nineteenth-century predecessors at Harvard would have accepted. The real transformation of the metaphor came through the historical imagination of his young colleague Perry Miller and the political savvy of Harvard graduate John F. Kennedy. By the time of their deaths a few weeks apart in 1963, the scholar and the statesman had left behind a city more secularized, politicized and malleable than ever before.

Miller was born in Chicago in 1905, the son of staunch New Englanders. His mother was a distant relative of Mary Baker Eddy, the founder of the Christian Science movement. His father came west to attend Hillsdale College in Michigan to prepare to be a medical doctor. Perry entered the University of Chicago in 1922 but left after only a year to experience something of the world. He later said he envied the generation just ahead of him that had fought in the Great War. As a wandering man, he tried his hand at everything from acting to the merchant marine. He travelled to Colorado, New York City, Mexico,

Europe and Africa, ending up in the Belgian Congo. He finally returned to the University of Chicago, completed his undergraduate degree, and began the graduate studies that would lead him to Harvard and a distinguished career as a teacher, mentor and author. His impact on the field of American intellectual history is almost impossible to overestimate.

Perhaps even more than Morison, Miller set out to correct the dour image of the Puritans popularized in the 1920s by the journalist H. L. Mencken and the historian James Truslow Adams, among others. That Miller should have taken on this role is a bit odd in light of his own atheism. Nevertheless, he infused the study of American Puritanism with a new vitality and respectability, making it even fashionable. According to his friend, the neo-orthodox theologian Reinhold Niebuhr, Miller rescued a generation of democratic Americans from their collective 'embarrassment' over their autocratic Puritan forebears. His scepticism about human nature made him a 'believing unbeliever', a sort of Calvinist without the Calvinism. His histories were 'therapeutic', Niebuhr wrote.[7] Miller himself acknowledged in a review of one of Niebuhr's books in 1958 that he was among the 'atheists for Niebuhr' chided by philosophy professor Morton White for 'hav[ing] copiously availed themselves of Niebuhr's conclusions without pretending to share his basic and, to him, indispensable premise'.[8] In other words, Miller – along with Arthur Schlesinger, Jr., and other public intellectuals – wanted all the analytical power of a theology of original sin without believing any of it. As Morton charged, 'atheists for Niebuhr' reduced religion to an 'insight into man's nature'.[9]

By Miller's own account, his lifetime of scholarship devoted to the Puritans amounted to nothing less than a 'mission'. That mission came to him at the age of 21 while he was in the Congo. 'I came there seeking "adventure"', he wrote of his encounter with the bustling seaport of Matadi. There, Miller witnessed the unloading of drums of 'case oil' (kerosene) that had arrived from the 'inexhaustible wilderness of America' – the wilderness that the Puritan mind on its errand had so deeply penetrated and transformed.[10] One of his students later counted this story among the fabrications Miller invented to compensate for 'an existentialist fear of the void' in his restless life.[11] If that was so, then Miller read a powerful mission back into his own beginnings at the same time that he read a driving national mission back into the Puritan origins. He described his own calling as a struggle to account for the 'innermost propulsion of the United States'.[12] On that quest, he remade the Puritans' city beyond any of the nationalizing and politicizing it had undergone to date.

Miller's first book, *Orthodoxy in Massachusetts* (1933) did not comment on the Model of Christian Charity. That effort would begin a few years later and continue for the rest of his life and into his posthumous publications. In 1938, Miller produced a large anthology of Puritan writings. He co-edited the thick volume with Thomas H. Johnson, a teacher at the prestigious Lawrenceville School near Princeton, New Jersey, and dedicated it to his former Harvard professor, Samuel Eliot Morison. 'Much that the Puritans wrote has been deservedly forgotten', the editors admitted, 'but the dust has gathered as well upon the works of some who, when brought into the light of the present, appear to have been powerful instruments in working out the social and political, as well as the religious and cultural, destiny of America'. They set out to rescue from obscurity these 'powerful instruments' in the world of ideas and to show how they helped set the trajectory of the nation's 'destiny'. Miller and Johnson placed Winthrop's discourse as the first entry in a section called 'The Theory of the State and Society'. Classified in this way, Winthrop's 'lecture or lay-sermon' emphasized the 'civil government' side of his task as much as the religious, and that is what the editors intended.[13] Set in this context, however, the discourse was read for decades to come as, first and foremost, a work of political theory or statecraft. That selective reading meant that only one part of Winthrop's vision, admittedly an important part, would come to serve for the whole at the expense of the governor's wider concerns. Their source for the document, of which they included a little less than half, was the new edition published in 1931 by the Massachusetts Historical Society in the second volume of *The Winthrop Papers*, to this day the most authoritative and best-annotated version available. Miller and Johnson's anthology, reissued as a two-volume paperback in the 1960s, became ubiquitous on America's college campuses in history, religion and literature classes.

While generations of students learned about the Model of Christian Charity in the pages of this book, they did not learn precisely how to interpret it from this popular source. For that, we have to turn to Miller's wider scholarship and trace what he did to the city on a hill in these landmark books. Given where Miller had placed the Model in his anthology, it is not surprising that he employed Winthrop's discourse as a means to understand the 'Puritan state'. And he did so specifically as an outworking of an 'idea', a tendency consistent with the pre-eminence he gave to the power of thought in shaping the world. In *The New England Mind*, published in 1939, he claimed that Winthrop pictured himself as 'another Moses in a new Deuteronomy' who, in the Model of Christian Charity, 'outlined in advance the basis of New England politics'. That basis was a community bound together by love, the very point his teacher Morison had stressed at the beginning of the decade. But here Miller went beyond his mentor to claim that 'New England political theory made the state almost a kind of second incarnation, a Messiah fathered by God and born of the people'. This is a weighty metaphor loaded with implications for how Americans ought to understand the Puritans. Rightly or wrongly, Miller hitched the theme of America's Messianic consciousness to the city on a hill.[14] Those who relied on Miller would later make that connection even more explicit, even when they did not acknowledge their debt to him.

In the 1940s, war service took Miller away from Cambridge as it did Morison and so many other professors and students. He was stationed in England with the US Office of Strategic Services, the precursor to the CIA. Upon his return to Harvard in 1945, he resumed his study of the Puritans and their legacy. In a lecture on Jonathan Edwards in 1949 at Bennington College in Vermont, Miller looked again at Winthrop's shipboard discourse.

This time, he isolated the phrases that have since come to epitomize the Model of Christian Charity. Up to this point, the 'city on a hill' had not yet become the automatic, most succinct way to explain the document, its author and the Puritan project. But here in 1949 we can witness the process well underway of whittling down the Model to a few quotable words. Retaining the original spelling, Miller wrote: 'On the voyage over, in 1630, John Winthrop said to them: "For wee must Consider that wee shall be as a Citty vppon a Hill, the eies of all people are vppon us".' This was the kind of shorthand approach to the Model – now typical – that historians over the previous century had not attempted. How much meaning and significance Miller managed then to read into these few words is striking. The ruling elite among the Puritan emigrants intended nothing less than to lead an exportable revolution. From the whole prodigious output of Puritan divines and statesmen, Miller extracted two phrases that now constituted the mission statement for a revolutionary city on a hill: 'They had been attempting in England to lead a revolution; after the King's dismissal of Parliament in 1629 it looked as though there was no longer any hope of revolution there, and so they migrated to New England, to build the revolutionary city, where they could exhibit to Englishmen an England that would be as all England should be'.[15]

In a 1952 lecture at Brown University, Miller continued to explore the Model in the context of the Puritans' mission. The added dimension here came from Miller's effective use of metaphors, adding military jargon on top of the biblical and Puritan city on a hill. The world of battlefield operations well known to this veteran permeated his description. It was as if a pushpin marked the city on a hill on a map at Eisenhower's headquarters. In a single paragraph, Miller used the words 'maneuver', 'task force', and 'flank attack'. Today, we use the phrase 'task force' so often in politics, business and academia that we forget its origin in the Second World War, first in naval operations as a name for a temporary unit under a single commander sent out on special assignment. Since later historians would repeat many of these ideas and even use Miller's metaphors, the whole section is worth quoting: 'Winthrop and his colleagues . . . could see in the pattern of history that their errand was not a mere scouting expedition: it was an essential maneuver in the drama of Christendom. The Bay Company was not a battered remnant of suffering Separatists thrown up on a rocky shore; it was an organized task force of Christians, executing a flank attack on the corruptions of Christendom. These Puritans did not flee to America; they went in order to work out that complete reformation which was not yet accomplished in England and Europe, but which would quickly be accomplished if only the saints back there had a working model to guide them'. The evocative power of this picture just a few years after the war is undeniable. Miller's mobilized Puritans would scramble onto the shore, implement their strategy for an 'ideal polity', gain indispensable experience on the ground with instituting that form of government, and stand ready with a 'working model' to be called to England's assistance.[16]

How evident this mission had been to ordinary colonists back in 1630 was another matter, Miller acknowledged. Most settlers might have been conscious only of the surface intention of their divine vocation. They might have seen themselves only as part of a plan to build a godly church and state in the New World. But Winthrop understood the mission behind the mission, Miller claimed, although it sounded more like Miller was the one blessed with a special gnosis. Key to that understanding was Winthrop's confidence that he could discern the hand of God in current events. Miller extracted this conviction from the text of the Model. As a city on a hill, with the world's eyes on it, the Puritan colony would 'vindicate' God's cunning work in the world. The city was being built to advance the Reformation in its purest form, a model so powerful 'that ultimately all Europe would imitate New England'. On that goal Winthrop fixed his vision. Or perhaps we should say that here Miller took one more step toward reinventing the city on a hill as a blueprint for world revolution. New England's success, he added, would show the 'Calvinist internationale' how to finish the 'revolution in Europe' – an odd bit of Cold

War hyperbole that turned Puritanism into a seventeenth-century preview of global revolutionary ideology.[17] When the second volume of *The New England Mind* appeared the next year, Miller used the same military metaphors and global mission statement he had adopted in his lectures. Mixing his own commentary with paraphrases from the Model, Miller claimed that 'The migration was no retreat from Europe: it was a flank attack. We are to be a city set upon a hill, the eyes of all the world are upon us; what we succeed in demonstrating, Europe will be bound to imitate, even Rome itself'. Armed with this transformational mission, the Puritans were anything but 'refugees seeking a promised land'. They looked to the day of triumph over their enemies back in the Old World.[18] If Winthrop knew the Puritan mission better than his fellow passengers, Miller knew it best of all.

Miller's short life was marred by depression and alcoholism. He died of heart failure in 1963 at the age of 58, just weeks after John F. Kennedy's assassination, reportedly grief-stricken over the president's death. His widow published some of the essays he left behind.[19] Among these is one further notable reflection on John Winthrop, his Model of Christian Charity, and the metaphor of the city on a hill. The 'Puritan definition of purpose', he wrote, was so clearly and powerfully defined at the colony's founding and then had reached so far across the opening West that it had shaped the consciousness of an entire nation and continued to absorb every immigrant into its ideal no matter how diverse his background. The effort to nationalize the Puritan origins of America, begun in the early nineteenth century and evident in Peleg Sprague, Tocqueville, and Bancroft, continued into the 1960s. In Miller's way of telling the story, Winthrop addressed a ship full of 'proto-Americans'. This was nothing less than a community spoken into being by the power of the word. To be one of these exceptional Americans meant to recommit oneself day by day to the ideas that made and sustained a people with a mission. That identity would not necessarily make Americans popular. Indeed, 'one can argue that coming down from this Puritan conception of America's unique destiny – "Wee must consider," said Winthrop, "that wee shall be as a Citty vpon a Hill, the eies of all people [are] vppon us" – has descended that glib American phrase, "God's country", which so amuses when it does not exasperate our allies'. But Miller thought that later generations of New Englanders failed to adapt this idea of the national covenant to changing circumstances as they prospered and grew. They did not have their forebears' capacity of will and decisive action.[20]

As a measure of the degree to which the city on a hill had been remade by the late 1950s we need look no further than the University of Chicago professor and Librarian of Congress Daniel Boorstin. Boorstin noted the transformation of the study of Puritanism from the days of Parrington to the 'scholars at the old Puritan stronghold, Harvard' – namely, Samuel Eliot Morison, Perry Miller and Kenneth Murdock. Boorstin wrote an important three-volume study of American life called simply *The Americans*, the first volume of which appeared in 1958. He entitled part one 'A City Upon a Hill'. It is doubtful that any previous generation of historians would have thought to begin the story of America so explicitly in this way. He started his trilogy on America with the voyage of the *Arbella*. This moment now served as America's point of origin. He called John Winthrop's words nothing less than the 'keynote of American history'. This is the exalted role it was now possible to assign to the city on a hill, a phrase ignored by historians for so many years. 'No one writing after the fact, three hundred years later', he added, 'could better have expressed the American sense of destiny'. Here in 1958 we have a way of articulating the meaning and significance of the city on a hill that is commonplace more than 50 years later. We have in place the now-orthodox way of interpreting the city, as we will see much more clearly in the following chapters. 'The Puritan beacon for misguided mankind was to be neither a book nor a theory', Boorstin continued. 'It was to be the community itself. America had something to teach all men: not by precept but by example, not by what it said but by how it lived'.[21] In the metaphor's curious fate, only half the meaning the Christian tradition had given to Matthew 5.14 survived. Down to and including the Puritans, the vulnerable city had been a call to Christians to watch their doctrine and life. For some, for whom America was an idea or a proposition, that city would come to embody a doctrine without a way of life. For Boorstin, that symbol almost embodied a way of life without a doctrine. Perry Miller's community built by the word was for Boorstin a community built by the deed. Either way, in profession or practice, exemplary or revolutionary, the city on a hill embodied America by the end of the 1950s.

In 1965, the prolific Samuel Eliot Morison, now in his late seventies, wrote a new textbook of American history, the 1,100-page *Oxford History of the American People*. He carried the whole story down to Kennedy's assassination and ended with the words and music to the song 'Camelot' from the 1960 Lerner and Loewe musical:

> Don't let it be forgot
> That once there was a spot
> For one brief shining moment
> That was known as Camelot.[22]

It was as if American history itself had come to a halt in 1963 by the hand of Lee Harvey Oswald. All we could do was wait for the return from Avalon of the 'once and future king'.

Morison brought his panorama of America full circle by beginning and ending with Kennedy. Early in the book, the slain president's name appeared linked to none other than John Winthrop, the Puritan mission, and the Model of Christian Charity. As they anticipated building their 'New Canaan', Morison wrote, these idealistic 'immigrants' believed 'that they were "a city upon a hill," "with the eyes of all people" upon them; an example to prove that it was possible to lead the New Testament life, yet make a living'. The footnote then directed the reader to a modern speech. It was almost as if the modern use of these words added significance to the earlier use. If not, then Morison's note seems arbitrary. Unintentionally, though, he cited the precise moment when the modern political history of America as the city on a hill began. Morison noted that the Model of Christian Charity, the document he had brought back into print a half-century before, had been 'quoted by President-elect John F. Kennedy in his speech to the General Court of Massachusetts, 9 January 1961. . ' [23]

That farewell, known for a time as JFK's 'City on a Hill' speech, launched the biblical, Puritan metaphor into contemporary American politics and culture. This powerful symbol, now so closely identified with the populist Right, entered modern American politics as an emblem of the internationalist Left. In crafting this pre-inaugural speech, Kennedy's aide and speechwriter, Ted Sorensen, remade the city on a hill. With a rhetorical wizardry unmatched in America history, a half-Jewish, Scandinavian Unitarian from Nebraska took a full-blooded Irish Catholic from Boston and grafted him into the stock planted and tended for more than 300 years by the Puritan Brahmins. From that moment in the Massachusetts State House in 1961 down to Ronald Reagan, the nation heard the 'Winthrop message' via the 'Kennedy message'.

Exactly why Sorensen decided to use Winthrop and the city on a hill remains unknown. In September 2009, a year or so before his death, I asked the speechwriter how he first encountered the Model of Christian Charity. Perhaps he had been assigned it in a history or literature course at the University of Nebraska in the 1940s? Perhaps he had even read it in Perry Miller's anthology? Always careful to ascribe the President's speeches to Kennedy and not to himself, Sorensen simply replied, 'I have no recollection whatsoever how that came across my desk before it was used by JFK in his January 1961 pre-inaugural address [F]arewell to Massachusetts'. The idea could have originated with Kennedy himself, of course, who had earned his degree in government from Harvard in 1940. But his transcripts show no record of his having taken classes with Morison or Miller. The name

'Winthrop' may not have signified more to him than the residence hall where he got into trouble for entertaining women after hours. Sorenson's memoirs, published in 2008, left no other clues. He explained only that the precedent for this speech was Abraham Lincoln's farewell to Springfield, Illinois, a century before.[24]

To some degree, the image of the city on a hill was present in the Kennedy campaign as early as the 1960 race. In May, Henry Luce's *Life* magazine began a series of articles, combining text and full-colour photographs, on the theme of 'The National Purpose'. The editor who had coined the phrase 'The American Century' chose his words carefully. The full-page photo that opened the lavishly illustrated series showed the marble-clad interior of the National Archives in Washington, DC. The caption called the building the 'Shrine of the Founding Scriptures' and showed reverent visitors viewing the holy relics of the Declaration of Independence, the Constitution and the 'creed' of the Bill of Rights. Other illustrations depicted the Mayflower Compact, the Federalist Papers, the Monroe Doctrine, William Lloyd Garrison's *Liberator*, the Gettysburg Address, FDR's 'Four Freedoms' speech and the 1945 United Nations Charter, the preamble of which 'marked acceptance by the world of principles originally laid down in the Declaration of Independence'.[25] Luce's notion of national purpose reached global proportions. Contributors over the next few months included evangelist Billy Graham and political theorists Clinton Rossiter and Walter Lippmann. For those in search of a grand narrative, this was about as grand as they came.

Life later asked party nominees Richard Nixon and John F. Kennedy to extend the series as the presidential election neared. Senator Kennedy's essay was entitled 'We must climb to the hilltop'. The Democratic candidate defined the national purpose vaguely, as any cautious campaigner might do so close to election day, as a constant 'aspiring, struggling, striving and searching', an ongoing experiment, a never-ending quest – toward what exactly he never said. All nations strive, he wrote, but America was exceptional in its 'strong sense of destiny', its optimism, and its 'willing[ness] to experiment'. 'New frontiers', he added, in words that soon came to define his presidency, 'have always seemed unfolding on our horizons'. He called on the nation to leave the 'valley' of complacency. 'Now it is time once again to climb to the hilltop, to be reinvigorated and reinspired by those faraway peaks, the principles that are vital to our national greatness, that underlie our national purpose, that foster our "American dream".'[26]

In Kennedy's farewell to the Massachusetts legislature as president-elect five months later, the inspiring view from the top of the dreamy hilltop became the view that others had as they looked to the Bay State. Early in the eight-minute speech, Kennedy introduced the theme of Massachusetts' 'democratic institutions' as 'beacon lights for other nations as well as our sister states'. 'For what Pericles said to the Athenians', he continued, 'has long been true of this commonwealth: "We do not imitate – for we are a model to others".' He then carefully situated himself within the ever-expanding citizenship that had continuously remade Boston and its mission since the seventeenth century. 'The enduring qualities of Massachusetts – the common threads woven by the Pilgrim and the Puritan, the fisherman and the farmer, the Yankee and the immigrant – will not be and could not be forgotten in this nation's executive mansion'. In contemplating the daunting responsibilities facing him as president, he continued, 'I have been guided by the standard John Winthrop set before his shipmates on the flagship Arbella three hundred and thirty-one years ago, as they, too, faced the task of building a new government on a perilous frontier'. And then he quoted the truncated phrases from the Model of Christian Charity that by 1961 had become the accepted shorthand for the whole complex meaning of the Puritan mission. '"We must always consider", [Winthrop] said, "that we shall be as a city upon a hill – the eyes of all people are upon us"'.

But what exactly did that city stand for in Kennedy's mind? Was it a holy commonwealth free at last to observe the purity of the ordinances of God's

Word? Was it a haven for English Protestants fleeing from a king and an archbishop too cozy with Catholicism? Was it a spectacle to a watching world of a community knit together by the bonds of brotherly affection that placed public need above private ambition? Was it a revolutionary city armed to complete the Reformation and launch a mission to transform England and the rest of Europe? Obviously, the Catholic Kennedy could not conjure up all or even many of the historical meanings embedded in or ascribed to the city on a hill. It could not signify for him what it had for the Puritans. Instead, he used it as a metaphor for something quite mundane: ethical government. The corrupt Massachusetts legislature was meant to take note, as Kennedy set the tone for his administration: 'Today the eyes of all people are truly upon us – and our governments, in every branch, at every level, national, state and local, must be as a city upon a hill – constructed and inhabited by men aware of their great trust and their great responsibilities'. Government itself now sat perched as the city on a hill.

Only once more did Kennedy invoke the hilltop city. On 7 June 1961, after addressing the graduating class at Annapolis earlier that day, he told a meeting of the Big Brothers of America, 'I feel we are a city on a hill and that one of our great responsibilities during these days is to make sure that we in this country set an example to the world not only of helping and assisting them to fulfill their own destiny, but also demonstrating what a free people can do'. Echoing the famous plea from his Inaugural Address for Americans to ask what they can do for their country, the president urged his audience to continue to serve their communities in ordinary ways. The city on a hill represented the nation's spirit of public service. Beyond these instances, the image of the city on a hill never came to define his presidency the way it would Ronald Reagan's. Fifty years later, other Kennedys in public office would try to resurrect the public's memory of JFK's pre-Reagan claim to the city on a hill, but the odds of overcoming Reagan's successful use of the metaphor seemed slim to none at all.

When Morison came to his textbook account of Kennedy's fateful visit to Dallas, Texas, on 22 November 1963, he quoted a few lines from the speech the president was set to deliver that day. In the last paragraph of the speech his Lone Star audience never heard, Kennedy drew a metaphor from the prophet Ezekiel to call America the 'watchmen on the walls of world freedom'. Turning to the second chapter of the Gospel of Luke and to Psalm 127, he said that he hoped the nation might 'achieve in our time and for all time the ancient vision of "peace on earth, good will toward men". 'That must always be our goal', he concluded, '– and the righteousness of our cause must always underlie our strength. For as was written long ago: "except the Lord keep the city, the watchman waketh but in vain".[27]

Whether Perry Miller shaped Kennedy's handling of the city on a hill remains unknown. But together the historian and the politician changed how the nation read the Model of Christian Charity and interpreted the city on a hill. Kennedy's role in the metaphor's rapid rise to national prominence was evident almost immediately. In 1962, one historian was now able to refer to the 'often quoted' words from the Model of Christian Charity – a trend that began with Kennedy. Showing Miller's influence, the author then wrote that the city on a hill 'epitomizes the cosmic scale of Winthrop's thinking and the militance of his temper in 1630. . . . [B]y colonizing America [the Puritans] were making no retreat. Rather, they were setting up a model of the kind of state they hoped to see soon in England'.[28] Also in 1962, another historian placed Winthrop's idea of the city among 'the most-quoted phrases of Puritan literature' – hardly something any previous generation of Americans could have said. Kicking Miller up a notch, he then drew the kind of straight line through history that *Life* magazine had attempted with such bravado in 1960, though without *Life*'s civic boosterism: 'The sense that they are a peculiar people, designed by Providence to live in a more perfect community than any known in the Old World, the sense that it is America's mission to set an example to other nations, is part of America's Puritan inheritance. It echoes through the *Battle Hymn of the Republic*, the Gettysburg Address, and the crusade to make the world safe for democracy. At its worst it becomes the vulgar, naïve, chauvinistic idealism of the innocent abroad and the *Quiet American*.[29] Apparently, the Puritan mission had propelled the United States all the way into the jungles of Vietnam. Whatever truth there is in that claim, and there may be much, it was the biblical metaphor of the city that was expected to tie it all together into one story. In 1963, Miller's friend Reinhold Niebuhr, along with co-author Alan Heimert, traced America's 'messianic consciousness' to the Enlightenment and before that to 'the millenarian impulse of New England Puritan belief, in the words of John Winthrop, that they were like "a city set upon a hill," a colony whose errand was to establish a pattern for all Christendom so the Reformation would be fulfilled'.[30] By the time of Kennedy's death, it had become possible to make the fragmentary phrase 'city on a hill' stand all by itself for the nation's messianic impulse. The thesis and the very words are Perry Miller's.[31]

Not every historian in the 1960s thought in these terms, of course. Indeed, in important ways the 'silence' noticed in the nineteenth century was still possible in the mid-twentieth century, despite Kennedy, Sorensen and the Harvard faculty. In 1968, intellectual historian Lee Tuveson published *Redeemer Nation: The Ideal of America's Millennial Role*, a classic study of America's Messianic identity that has not been surpassed.[32] But Tuveson never used the city on a hill, the Model of Christian Charity, or even John Winthrop to account for the United States' self-understanding as a Christ among nations. This omission is hardly imaginable today. Less than 45 years ago, the 'city on a hill' was still not an inescapable part of America's Messianic identity.

After Kennedy's assassination, other politicians were slow to adopt the city on a hill as the definitive metaphor for America. Invocations of it in presidential rhetoric remained rare. In a speech in Boston in 1964, President

Lyndon B. Johnson quoted from the Winthrop section of Kennedy's farewell to the Massachusetts legislature and re-affirmed America as a spectacle to the world. 'Those who watch us,' the Texas Democrat said, '. . . see burning in the midst of the city a light of freedom, a flame of the spirit, the brightness of the nobility which is in man, and the arms of the Statue of Liberty awaiting them'. The following year, Robert F. Kennedy incorporated his slain brother's metaphor in a speech before an ecumenical gathering in Chicago of the National Council of Christians and Jews. Confronting the problem of racial discrimination North and South, the former Attorney General called on Americans to live up to their ideals. The 'city upon the hill' remained the nation's destination, a goal not yet reached. Like the seafaring Puritans, 'we are still in the middle of our journey'. Confronted by continuing racial injustice, we are 'only halfway to the city upon the hill'.[33] Republicans also picked up the metaphor. In a speech in 1971 in New York City before the Knights of Columbus, the Catholic fraternal order, the Quaker Richard Nixon recognized the biblical origins of Winthrop's metaphor. 'Think how presumptuous that was to say then,' he reflected. 'America, not even settled, a few colonists just about to arrive, and here he said, "You are the light of the world. A city set upon a hill cannot be hidden". That was the spirit that made this country'. He hoped the nation would continue to match its material strength with such spiritual strength as exemplified by the Puritans.

From obscurity in 1930, when the *Christian Science Monitor* failed to quote it, the city on a hill achieved a degree of prominence in the 1960s as a secular, political metaphor. Politicians and historians gave shape to it largely in the liberal, Democratic political culture of that decade. The literal words on the page of Winthrop's discourse remained what they had been for over 300 years. With only slight variation, they still matched the Model of Christian Charity and the Geneva translation of the New Testament. But while the phrase remained the same on the surface, it had been filled with a new content and put to new uses. The metaphor now signified something it had not pointed to before, something beyond Jesus and Winthrop. America's preoccupation with the city on a hill as a national myth did not emerge in the 1960s as something wholly new but rather as old words deployed in a new way, with a new purpose, causing the nation and eventually other nations to hear those words in an unprecedented way. But this 'repurposed' metaphor would not carry echoes of Camelot much longer. Before the decade was out, a rising political star in California took the city he encountered in the 1960s and made it his own shining city.

6

The shining city, 1969–1989

. . . [I]n my mind it was a tall proud city built on rocks stronger than oceans, wind-swept, God-blessed, and teeming with people of all kinds living in harmony and peace, a city with free ports that hummed with commerce and creativity, and if there had to be walls, the walls had doors and the doors were open to anyone with the will and the heart to get here. That's how I saw it, and see it still.

RONALD REAGAN'S FAREWELL, 1989

On the first page of his 2009 book, *The Myth of American Exceptionalism*, British historian Godfrey Hodgson took aim at Ronald Reagan. The Republican president's repeated use of John Winthrop's Model of Christian Charity to capture a certain brand of American exceptionalism bothered the Oxford University professor. Hodgson rightly noted the 'anachronism' of making the Puritan governor a proto-American and a prophet of the future glory of the United States. He concluded that 'the sermon that Winthrop preached and the sermon that Ronald Reagan used to inspire a conservative shift in American politics some 350 years later have virtually nothing in common'.[1] Historian John Patrick Diggins had raised a similar concern a few years before Hodgson. After careful study, he concluded that Reagan's theology had little to do with seventeenth-century Calvinist views of God's sovereignty, man's depravity and Christianity's call to a life of repentance and self-denial. Indeed, Reagan's optimism aligned him more closely with Ralph Waldo Emerson and the Transcendentalists' Over Soul than with anything resembling Puritanism.[2]

The distance across the centuries separating Reagan from Winthrop does indeed raise important reminders about the difference between the past as experienced and the past as remembered and recycled for purposes previous generations could not have imagined. The space that opens up in our mental picture of American history once we put Winthrop back in his own time allows us to know something important about Winthrop, but it also allows us to see and hear things in Reagan's rhetoric we might otherwise miss. While historical distance makes Winthrop less familiar to us, it simultaneously makes Reagan less familiar as well. That unfamiliarity can bring fresh insights. Tracking Reagan's use of Winthrop, especially his now famous biblical and Puritan metaphor of the 'city on a hill', reveals how the chief executive functioned in the 1980s in his role as what some have called the 'high priest' of America's civil religion. Doing so also shows further how Christians in America lost ownership of one of their key metaphors. Ironically, American evangelicals' favourite president did more than any other figure in history to take a piece of their Christian identity from them.

That biblical/national metaphor, picked up somewhere along the way in the 1960s by the former Democrat turned Goldwater conservative, served Reagan well for 20 years. As early as 1952, Reagan had claimed that America was 'less of a place than an idea'. And that idea became a storyline that brought clarity to his version of American history. In George Mason University professor Hugh Heclo's judgement, Reagan as president became a 'narrator, a teller of many stories that all served to expound and defend what he regarded as the one American story'.[3] The city on a hill seemed ready-made to fit into that larger narrative.

The picture of America as a chosen, duty-bound, light-bearing city clearly inspired Reagan as did few other ideas. But it is also true that in countless speeches between 1969 and 1989 Reagan remade the metaphor by a process of addition and subtraction. He tacked the adjective 'shining' onto the city at some point. But more significantly, he also removed the last traces of the city's ancient Christian and later English Puritan nuances. Indeed, the phrase 'city on a hill', originating in the Gospel of Matthew and understood for hundreds of years as a metaphor of the church and its pastoral ministry, sounds the way it does to twenty-first century Americans, and gets debated within the framework it does, because of Reagan, not because of Jesus or Winthrop or Kennedy. So successful was the Republican president in putting his trademark upon it that his fellow citizens, including most historians and journalists, soon forgot that president-elect Kennedy had introduced Winthrop's image into American presidential rhetoric. The city on a hill Americans debate today is the Republican icon's invention. More than any other modern figure, Reagan transformed Jesus' metaphor into a political slogan inseparable from the 1980s 'Reagan Revolution' and from that movement's legacy in the Republican Party. Today, Republican candidates on the local, state and national levels, from aspiring small-town mayors to Sarah Palin, use it incessantly to attach themselves to Reagan's image in the conservative mind. Its political use has been potent enough to all but eclipse its biblical meaning, even among American Christians who might reasonably be expected to resent seeing their metaphor dressed up like Uncle Sam.

In his autobiography, published the year after he left the Oval Office, Reagan made one passing reference to John Winthrop. Recalling the last year of his first term as president in 1984, he wrote of his conviction at the time that America 'had begun the process of spiritual revival that was so badly needed'. By a 'spiritual revival' Reagan did not mean repentance, conversion, or awakening as understood by Christian theology. Instead, he wrote of recapturing a 'special vision' – Winthrop's reminder to his fellow colonists 'that they had the opportunity to create a new civilization based on freedom unlike any other before it, a unique and special "shining city on a hill".'[4] Yet Reagan's emphasis on freedom and a new civilization had less to do with Winthrop's original purpose for his colony than with Thomas Paine's revolutionary rhetoric. Paine was Reagan's favourite among the Founders, and he quoted the patriot's belief that America in 1776 had the capacity to 'begin the world over again' about as often as he quoted Winthrop. Nevertheless, this sole reference to Winthrop in the former president's memoirs little indicated the hold the city on a hill had on his imagination.

Reagan's earliest known use of it came in October 1969 during the first of his two terms as governor of California. During his career as a public speaker, Reagan had begun to jot on note cards quotable phrases from historical figures ranging from Emma Lazarus to Vladimir Lenin. On one of these cards, Reagan wrote down his much-used quotation from Winthrop's Model of Christian Charity.[5] The discourse had been widely available since Perry Miller's anthology appeared in the 1930s, and the actor-turned-politician could easily have encountered it in any number of places. Kennedy had already quoted from it in 1961, and Lyndon Johnson and Robert Kennedy had invoked the same passages in 1964. The occasion for Reagan's 1969 speech, and Winthrop's likely debut in his political rhetoric, was a fundraising event in Washington, D.C., for the fledgling Eisenhower College, a liberal arts institution in Seneca Falls, New York, founded four years earlier. With Vietnam War protestors very much on his mind (he had faced them at UC–Berkeley as California's governor), Reagan appealed in his speech for a renewal of individual character to save American civilization. He varied the text only slightly from his handwritten note card, adding the definite article 'the' in front of 'people' and 'all' in front of 'the world': 'We shall be as a city upon a hill. The eyes of all the people are upon us, so that if we shall deal falsely with our God in this work we have undertaken and so cause Him to withdraw His present help from us, we shall be made a story and a byword through all the world'.[6]

In light of how Reagan would handle this quotation over the next two decades, a few things stand out. Reagan had not yet added the word 'shining' to his city, and the quotation included Winthrop's warning of divine judgement, a shadow that would mostly vanish later. We can catch a glimpse of how Reagan would rework Winthrop's message in the future, by reading the next sentence of the California governor's appeal to potential donors: 'To you who are considering what you can do to support Eisenhower College, I tell you that without such schools, this shining dream of John Winthrop's may well become the taste of ashes in our mouths'.[7] The college did not survive beyond the early 1980s, but Winthrop's city had begun its path to prominence in the national consciousness.

Just over four years later, near the end of his second term as governor of California, Reagan addressed the first Conservative Political Action Conference (CPAC) in Washington, D.C. This annual event would become – and still is – a boot camp for young conservatives eager to be at their movement's epicenter. Reagan's 1974 speech, the first of a dozen he gave at CPAC between 1974 and 1988, included details about the setting for Winthrop's words that became stock elements in his narrative, among them the image of the 'tiny deck' of the *Arbella* and the common assumption that Winthrop delivered his sermon while aboard that ship and near America's shores. Not one of these historical details can be corroborated by surviving evidence. Nevertheless, the story of the courageous band of intrepid voyagers possessed a mythic quality that for Reagan transcended the literal events of 1630. They are the kinds of things repeated about the Puritans over the centuries in countless patriotic orations, and they have become a durable part of the story of America's founding. If they sound to cynics like the stuff of fable, it is important to remember that many popular college textbooks continue to repeat these same 'facts'.[8]

At this event in DC in 1974, as again in his 1975 CPAC appearance and in most of his subsequent uses of Winthrop, Reagan positioned the shining city near the end of his speech as a sort of summary call to covenantal obedience. For the time being, he retained Moses's and Winthrop's stern warning about the judgement that will fall upon the covenantal people who betray their God. In fact, in his 1975 CPAC speech he dropped the 'city on a hill' entirely and kept only the admonition not to 'deal falsely with our God' lest we become 'a story and a byword throughout the world'. Despite these sober words, Reagan never judged America guilty of this sin – not in the 1970s in the immediate wake of Watergate and Nixon's resignation, and not at any time in the future. 'We have *not* dealt falsely with our God', he reassured the assembled conservative activists in 1974, adding humorously, 'even if He *is* temporarily suspended from the classroom' – a reference to the Supreme Court's rulings a decade earlier against government-sponsored prayer and Bible reading in the nation's public schools. America remained faithful as the chosen nation. It had kept its side of the covenantal bargain and could therefore be assured of God's blessing. It had been a nation destined for 'world leadership' from the beginning. And in the disillusionment of the mid-1970s, Reagan believed, 'Americans are hungry to feel once again a sense of mission and greatness'.[9]

In 1976, the increasingly popular Reagan ran for the Republican nomination against President Gerald Ford. He failed to unseat the incumbent, but over the next four years he solidified and widened his base of supporters. Increasing frustration among voters with the economy and foreign policy under Jimmy Carter handed Reagan the perfect opportunity. Leading up to these two races in 1976 and 1980, Reagan refined his message week by week in his nationally syndicated radio spots. Called 'Viewpoint', the programme aired from January 1975 to October 1979 (with a break for several months while he campaigned in 1975 and 1976). Reagan wrote these short talks himself in longhand. They provide historians with instances of Reagan's thoughts and words unaltered by speechwriters and handlers.

In one radio address, taped on 7 August 1978, his account of the 'ideological struggle' then underway between communist totalitarianism and American freedom led him to the Puritan settlers who for him defined America's mission. His handwritten script reads: 'John Winthrop on the deck of the tiny Arbella in 1630 off the coast of Mass. said to the little band of pilgrims; "We shall be as a city upon a hill. The eyes of all people are upon us, so that if we shall deal falsely with our God in this work we have undertaken & so cause him to withdraw his present help from us, we shall be made a story & a byword throughout the world". 'This work', understood three centuries earlier by Winthrop as the task of securing liberty for Christians to worship God according to the 'ordinances' of Scripture and the dictates of conscience, had become a global revolutionary mission for Perry Miller and a call to ethical government and public service for John Kennedy. Now for Reagan it became an expression of modern political, economic and religious freedom and a tool of American anti-communism. 'The oath of the Communist Party U.S.A. written in 1930,' he added forebodingly, 'says nothing of a city upon a hill'.[10]

Reagan as presidential candidate in the run-up to the 1976 and 1980 elections refined his vision of America's national destiny. By the late 1970s he had stocked his rhetorical arsenal with quotations and metaphors assembled and reassembled in almost any order to capture America's providential calling and, more generally, to articulate America's civil religion. To Winthrop's city and Tom Paine's itch to 'begin the world over again', the Republican candidate added Franklin Roosevelt's 'rendezvous with destiny' and Pope Pius XII's belief that 'into the hands of America God has placed the destiny of an afflicted mankind'.[11] But in this eclectic group, Winthrop and his city remained the most consistent and predictable image in Reagan's narrative. When he announced his candidacy on 13 November 1979, for instance, he talked of Americans' faith in the future and indirectly criticized President Jimmy Carter's hand-wringing back in July about the nation's 'crisis of confidence'. Reagan rejected fatalism and any suggestion that there might be limits to prosperity, resources and national greatness. He blamed the overgrown, centralized federal government itself for the economic crisis of the 1970s. In this context, Reagan drew Winthrop's city into his battle to replace malaise with optimism. Tom Paine contributed his revolutionary rhetoric again and, sandwiched between two citations of FDR's 'rendezvous with destiny', Winthrop appeared once more 'on the deck of the tiny *Arbella*' to tell his 'little band of pilgrims' the now-familiar story of who they were. According to

Reagan, the world watched in 1979 to see if America would reach its destiny and 'become that shining city on a hill'.[12]

In an undated letter from some time after his November 13 announcement, Reagan explained to a pedantic correspondent who had quibbled with his failure to capitalize 'Pilgrim' why he called the Massachusetts Bay colonists 'pilgrims' at all. They were, of course, Puritans who, at least officially, remained within the Church of England, not the Separatists who settled Plymouth Colony and were later known to history as the Pilgrims. Historians, editors and politicians in the nineteenth century had used Puritan and Pilgrim almost interchangeably, as we have seen, but this distinction was not on Reagan's mind. He had his own purposes. 'I had simply used pilgrims with a small "p"', he wrote, 'meaning any such group of people who are embarked on a journey such as those who first came to this country. I just hadn't given thought to the fact that it might be translated to the particular group that were called Pilgrims among our Founding Fathers'. He thanked his correspondent, and promised that he would 'simply refer to them as a little band of travelers or whatever from now on'.[13] In other words, for Reagan, Winthrop and the Puritans mattered not for their exact identity in recorded history but for what they symbolized in his story of America. Even his wish to have them be 'a little band of travelers' simplifies a much more complicated reality. And Reagan soon returned to calling them 'Pilgrims', anyway.

Reagan the campaigner never missed an opportunity to talk about the city on a hill. In his televised national debate with independent candidate John Anderson during the 1980 race, the Republican hopeful ended his closing remarks by fusing Tom Paine and John Winthrop once again. 'I believe', he concluded, 'the people of this country can, and together, we can begin the world over again. We can meet our destiny – and that destiny [is] to build a land here that will be, for all mankind, a shining city on a hill. I think we ought to get at it'.[14]

Reagan, of course, went on to defeat both Anderson and Carter in November, and he carried Winthrop with him into the White House. More than 20 of his presidential speeches over the next eight years, from foreign policy addresses in 1981 to his last weekly radio address broadcast in 1989, mention the city on a hill in some way. The shining city became a fundamental part of his message of spiritual renewal, national pride, expanding opportunity, global democratic revolution and America's providential calling.

The shining city first of all stood for economic freedom and progress. Reagan made this point clear in a long luncheon speech to the World Affairs Council of Philadelphia in October 1981. He was about to travel to Mexico for a summit on economic development among poorer nations. Over the shouts of protesters, Reagan used Winthrop to define America as a land of freedom where individual initiative, hard work and perseverance find their certain reward. Free markets – stabilized by voluntary cooperation and the institutions of home, church and school, and helped along by a government that breaks down barriers – energize the economy and benefit everyone, he promised. A year later, speaking to the National League of Cities, the president tied Winthrop to domestic economic renewal and envisioned multiple vibrant cities dotting the land: 'America must once again be filled of leaders [like Winthrop] dedicated to building shining cities on hills, until our nation's future is bright again with their collective glow'.[15]

Second, Reagan envisioned the shining city as the point from which America's creed emanated to the world. On 3 October 1983, he addressed a banquet in Washington, D.C., celebrating the tenth anniversary of the Heritage Foundation, the conservative think tank that had done so much to promote the Reagan Revolution through its policy initiatives. He zeroed in on the 'democratic revolution underway' around the globe. In dealing with the Soviet Union, he disavowed a negative policy of containment and called instead on the 'free world' to 'go on the offensive with a forward strategy for freedom'. America's mission was clear: 'we must present to the world not just an America that's militarily strong, but an America that is morally powerful, an America that has a creed, a cause, a vision of a future time when all peoples have the right to self-government and personal freedom'. This vision, he argued, resonated with America's oldest founding principles, a connection that led him once again, yes, to John Winthrop. To the familiar story of tiny boats and huddled bands, Reagan added what once had been commonplace in his citations of Winthrop but had since become rare and was about to disappear entirely: the warning of divine judgement against those who deal falsely with God. But, true to his upbeat message, the president declared America not guilty. 'America has not been a story or a byword. That small community of Pilgrims prospered and, driven by the dreams and, yes, by the ideas of the Founding Fathers, went on to become a beacon to all the oppressed and poor of the world'. Reagan asked his audience members to pledge that they would labour hard so that future generations would say that they 'did keep faith with our God'.[16]

As paradoxical as it may sound, Reagan believed that global democratic revolution defined political conservatism in the late twentieth century. That revolution would bring prosperity, freedom, peace and security to the world. And this raises a third meaning for the shining city embedded in the other two: America's divine calling summoned the nation to a universal and perpetual task. Winthrop's original warning to the Puritans to live obediently to the covenant before the eyes of a watching world in order not to bring shame on the cause of the Gospel was refracted through Reagan's prism into an expansive secular mission to the world. Man was born to be free. America had the divine mandate to make that freedom a reality. In a 4 July speech in Decatur, Alabama, in 1984, Reagan awkwardly compressed two of Winthrop's sentences into a global mission statement for America: 'We shall be as a shining city for all the world upon the hill'.[17] In 1986, after his summit in Iceland with Soviet President Mikhail Gorbachev, he called the American dream 'the oldest dream of humanity: the dream of peace and freedom, a dream that someday must belong to every man, woman, and child on Earth'.[18]

These examples could be multiplied many times over. But one speech in particular, given near the end of his presidency, reinforced and summarized all of the meanings Reagan had worked out for the shining city during his presidency, repeating them nearly in the chronological order in which he had developed them. The event was the opening rally for the August 1988 Republican national convention in New Orleans. Reagan had to persuade his supporters that his vice president, George H. W. Bush, was the safe and genuine successor to the Reagan Revolution. Near the end of his speech on 14 August, the president urged the GOP to remind voters of the party's 'vision'. In the few sentences that followed, Reagan gave perhaps his clearest explication of the city on a hill to date. He provided almost an outline of how he had defined the city in previous presidential speeches. The Republicans, he said, ought to spread their message of 'a future of economic growth and opportunity and democratic revolution and peace among nations'. He then emphasized America's 'destiny' and 'great calling' and appealed to the 'shining city', 'a city aglow with the light of human freedom, a light that someday will cast its glow on every dark corner of the world and on every age and generation to come'.[19] Here, then, were the three themes embodied in Reagan's city: economic growth and opportunity; democratic revolution and world peace; and America's global and eternal mission.

These meanings did not go uncontested in the 1980s. They might sound compatible with Kennedy's liberalism, but critics on the left attacked Reagan's appropriation of Winthrop. Writing immediately after the Republican triumph in November 1980, Richard Lingeman moodily pondered why Reagan had won. The ignorant American voters had disappointed the *Nation* columnist by how easily they had fallen for the 'aw-shucks' and 'folksy' Reagan. A fear-mongering huckster, the candidate had played to their self-pity, promised to 'make America feel good about itself again', and parlayed that seductive message into victory. 'Reagan is the man from the land of the happy ending', the liberal journalist complained, dismissing Reagan's cinematic version of the

American dream as superficial. What did that dream amount to? Only that 'America will be the shining "city upon a hill," Reagan's crib from a sermon by John Winthrop in 1630 on board the ship Arbella bound for the New World'. Paraphrasing from F. Scott Fitzgerald, Lingeman concluded that in voting for Reagan 'America has found its past again'. But that nostalgic version of the happy past would prove inadequate, he predicted, and 'the sadness will come'.[20]

Democratic politicians also mobilized against Reagan's blueprint for the city. During the 1984 campaign, New York Governor Mario Cuomo served as the point man for the Democrats' attack on the sitting president's shining metropolis. Cuomo not only had to take on a popular president but also had to rally support for the Democratic candidate, former vice president Walter Mondale. Invited to give the keynote address at the Democratic national convention in San Francisco in July, the governor called his friend Larry King, the talk-show host, for advice. King later recalled Cuomo reading the entire speech to him over the phone and then asking him what he thought of the strategy of going after the Winthrop metaphor. 'You like this "city on the hill" idea?' Cuomo asked, adding that he intended to attack the image and not the president. The convention expected him to be tough on their opponent, he said, 'But I always call him President Reagan in this speech. I never slam him personally'. King travelled to San Francisco and heard Cuomo deliver his speech in person. He remembered that as he stood there he 'knew that magic was happening that night'. 'Anybody standing in that audience knew it', he continued. 'They knew that a new figure had emerged on the American scene. The speech was delivered like a summation to the jury by a great trial lawyer . . .'.[21]

Cuomo's 'trial lawyer' prosecution of Reagan thrilled the convention audience that night. New York Times columnist William Safire called the speech 'a stunner'. Cuomo's opening salvo challenged the president's stewardship of the city. In his thick New York accent, he acknowledged that 'in many ways we are a shining city on a hill'. 'But the hard truth', he added, 'is that not everyone is sharing in this city's splendor and glory. A shining city is perhaps all the President sees from the portico of the White House and the veranda of his ranch, where everyone seems to be doing well'. 'But there's another city; there's another part to the shining city', he warned, ticking off the economic hardships still faced by many Americans in the prosperous '80s. In fact, he said, the American story was better described as a Dickensian 'Tale of Two Cities' than a 'Shining City on a Hill'. He accused Reagan of subscribing to a social Darwinist philosophy of 'survival of the fittest' that kept the city shining for the few and the powerful. Predictable as Cuomo's partisan strategy may have been, his astute use of Reagan's favourite image for America points to just how potent the symbol had become. Tellingly, Cuomo worked hard not to discredit the metaphor itself or to return it to the hands of his own Catholic Church but rather to reassure the electorate that the Democratic Party and its policies – and not the Republicans – would build 'one city, indivisible, shining for all its people'.[22]

Democrats continued their challenge to Reagan's city four years later in the 1988 presidential campaign. Just three weeks before Reagan's 14 August address to the Republican National Convention, Democratic nominee Michael Dukakis worked John Winthrop into his acceptance speech in Atlanta, Georgia. In contrast to individualist Reaganomics, the Bay State governor quoted his Bay Colony predecessor to highlight 'the idea of community': 'An idea', he said, 'that was planted in the New World by the first Governor of Massachusetts'. 'We must', Dukakis continued, quoting Winthrop loosely, 'love one another with a pure heart fervently. We must delight in each other, make each other's condition our own, rejoice together, mourn together, and suffer together . . . We must, he said, be knit together as one'. 'John Winthrop wasn't talking about material success', he cautioned. 'He was talking about a country where each of us asks not only what's in it for some of us, but what's good and what's right for all of us'.[23]

None of this criticism deterred Reagan from the metaphor. Indeed, he would continue to use it until he left office. The single use of the city on a hill cited most often today by historians, journalists and bloggers was nearly his last. His farewell address to the nation on 11 January 1989, offered his longest and most detailed justification for why he had invoked the shining city so often during his career. In this nationally televised address from the Oval Office, Reagan saved his discussion of Winthrop until the end, as had been his custom for decades. Repeating a common assumption, he claimed that John Winthrop had used the metaphor of the city 'to describe the America he imagined'. Winthrop was a 'freedom man', Reagan said. Then, in simple but poignant words, Reagan offered a parting vision of his city:

> I've spoken of the shining city all my political life, but I don't know if I ever quite communicated what I saw when I said it. But in my mind it was a tall proud city built on rocks stronger than oceans, wind-swept, God-blessed, and teeming with people of all kinds living in harmony and peace, a city with free ports that hummed with commerce and creativity, and if there had to be walls, the walls had doors and the doors were open to anyone with the will and the heart to get here. That's how I saw it, and see it still.[24]

Reagan called his city 'God-blessed', but it seems fair to say that his image of it was utterly secular, consisting of no more than a bustling, tolerant commercial enterprise – a Scottish Enlightenment vision closer to Adam Smith than Jesus. This picture bears little resemblance to what John Winthrop must have imagined for the future of his plantation in New England. His venture had been in part a commercial enterprise, but only in part. For good or ill, the Puritans' religious mission had vanished in Reagan's narrative. On the literal surface, the words of the metaphor had survived intact, but the underlying meaning had been lost. The metaphor had become an empty vessel into which Reagan and any other politician poured his or her own content. The metaphor may have been enriched in some ways, but it was impoverished in others.

Reagan's last weekly radio address, broadcast a few days after his televised farewell, reinforced just how far away from Winthrop – and Christ – he had carried the city. Devoid of any theological or historical content, *any* content became possible. The Puritan settlers, he claimed, had hoped to 'found a new world, a city upon a hill, a light to the nations'. And the metaphor obligated America to act. 'Those words and that destiny beckon to us still. Whether we seek it or not, whether we like it or not, we Americans are keepers of the miracles'.[25]

Reagan and his wife Nancy retired to their ranch in California in 1989. Republican and Democratic presidents, candidates and pundits continued to talk about America as the city on a hill, but more often than not in reference to Reagan himself rather than to Winthrop and rarely to Kennedy. Reagan had captured the metaphor. Democrats spoke respectfully of his city, not daring now to criticize a catchphrase so closely identified with the memory of a former president who soon seemed to belong to the American people as a whole and not to any particular party or agenda. Republicans and Democrats continued to fight over the creedal content of the city, but no one doubted that America was called to *be* that city. Thanks largely to Reagan, the metaphor had become as inseparable from the American identity as the Stars and Stripes, the 'Battle Hymn of the Republic' and the Statue of Liberty. As Reagan faded into the darkness of Alzheimer's, his metaphor became a holy relic of the American civil religion.

No event in the twenty-first century has made Reagan's identification with Winthrop's city clearer than his funeral service in 2004 at Washington's National Cathedral. Reagan died on 5 June of that year at the age of 93. President George W. Bush, visiting Paris when he received the news, spoke just after midnight the following day. In a simultaneously odd and fitting remark, he said that Reagan's 'work is done, and now a shining city awaits him'. The city on a hill had become heaven itself. Years before, Reagan and Nancy had worked out every detail of his ecumenical funeral service. Protestant, Catholic, Orthodox and Muslim clerics participated. Included among the 300 pages of carefully detailed plans was a role for Supreme Court Justice Sandra Day O'Connor, a Reagan appointee to the high court and the first women so honoured. Rabbi Harold Kushner, 1980s bestselling author of *When Bad Things Happen to Good People*, read from the prophet Isaiah, and then it was O'Connor's turn. The Reagans had asked her to read a few excerpts from none other than John Winthrop's Model of Christian Charity – namely, his quotation from the Old Testament prophet Micah ('What does the Lord require of you but to do justly, love mercy and to walk humbly with your God?') and his reference to the city on a hill, including the warning of divine judgement.[26]

Former Republican Senator John Danforth, an ordained Episcopal priest, officiated at Reagan's funeral. Between renditions of 'The Battle Hymn of the Republic' sung by the Armed Forces Choir and 'Amazing Grace' sung by Irish tenor Ronan Tynan, Danforth delivered his brief homily. His words of comfort invoked neo-orthodox theologian Reinhold Niebuhr's 'children of light' and numbered Reagan among the light-bearers. He never once mentioned Christ. Nevertheless, Senator Danforth noted that the choice of texts for his sermon (Matthew 5.14–16) was 'obvious'. After all, Reagan had often quoted Jesus' words from the Sermon on the Mount, albeit indirectly by way of Winthrop's discourse: 'You are the light of the world. A city set on a hill cannot be hid'. In Reagan's reading of history, Danforth perceived, Winthrop's city stood for America itself. And the former Senator accepted Reagan's projection of the modern American nation retrospectively back into Winthrop's discourse. 'Winthrop believed that the eyes of the world would be on America because God had given us a special commission, so it was our duty to shine forth'. Simply put, 'The Winthrop message became the Reagan message'.

Only gradually in the two decades between 1969 and 1989 had the 'Winthrop message' become the 'Reagan message'. That message – putting aside the question of whether its twentieth-century progressive optimism and materialism had any vestige of Winthrop left in it – could easily have become the 'Kennedy message' or perhaps even the 'Johnson message' as an emblem of liberal internationalism, the New Frontier, or the Great Society. But neither Kennedy, nor Johnson, nor Nixon, all of whom quoted from Winthrop's discourse, affixed the metaphor of the city on a hill onto America with Reagan's tenacity and brilliant success. Reagan was not the first to use it. He was certainly not the last. But he made it his own. And in making it his own, he remade it to a degree never before seen in American history.

Analysing the Reagan message is not easy. For one thing, his story was not always ideologically consistent or coherent. It was libertarian and New Deal; conservative and revolutionary; globalist and nationalist; populist and elitist. It waged the Cold War and at the same time crusaded for nuclear disarmament. It invoked John Winthrop, Tom Paine and Ralph Waldo Emerson – sometimes in the same paragraph. Consciously or not, Reagan tried to synthesize every element of the American identity – Puritan, Enlightenment and Romantic. In part because of this eclecticism, the former president became as mysterious and controversial as any chief executive in American history.

In interpreting the American identity for his generation, or at least for his political constituency, Reagan effectively deployed the 'city on a hill'. He found it useful in any number of settings, domestic and foreign. The metaphor seemed to speak to the heart of his civil religion. The phrase 'civil religion' can be thrown around casually by historians and political theorists, but used precisely it serves as an adequate label for two distinct but interrelated patterns in any modern nation's self-understanding. These patterns both appeared in Reagan. On the one hand, civil religion denotes a doctrinally vague theism of the sort found on US currency and in the Pledge of Allegiance. The Supreme Court once referred to this national affirmation of faith as 'ceremonial deism'. This god of America's civic ceremonies remains largely anonymous. He is not explicitly the Christian God of the Apostles Creed or the other historic confessions of faith. Anyone but an atheist can picture his own god during a presidential inauguration or a 4 July celebration. On the other hand, 'civil religion' can also mean a set of aspirations that define a nation as distinct among its peers, beliefs about who a people are that they raise to the level of doctrine within a national creed, including those documents that embody their beliefs and that serve as a kind of national scripture. In the case of the United States, these might include, and not without controversy, belief in democracy, religious tolerance, free-market economics and the separation of church and state, as well as a canonical set of documents that might include, again not without controversy, the Mayflower Compact, the Declaration of Independence, the Constitution and the Gettysburg Address. These are the ideals and texts Americans subscribe to in order to identify themselves and to unite themselves into one people. For those who understand America primarily as a nation dedicated to a proposition, as Lincoln described the United States in the midst of the Civil War, getting these dogmas of the national faith right – and getting right with these dogmas – becomes critically important.

Every president in American history has participated to some extent in the nation's civil religion. It is a question of degree. Here is where Reagan stands out. This is the context in which his favourite quotation from Winthrop makes the most sense. Though he quoted the Bible less often than other presidents – a surprising tendency given his vision of God's providential relationship with the United States – Reagan endowed America's civil religion with more 'doctrinal' content than did any other chief executive in history. Moreover, he served as the most successful high priest of that national liturgy.

At least this was the judgement of two university professors at the close of Reagan's presidency. In 1988, evangelical scholars Richard V. Pierard and Robert D. Linder compared various presidents' handling of civil religion. Pierard had been on record since 1970 as a critic of American evangelicalism's alliance with right-wing politics and the loss of its prophetic witness on behalf of social justice.[27] Pierard and his co-author began their critique of Reagan by looking at a passage from his eulogy for the American sailors killed aboard the USS *Stark* in the Persian Gulf in 1987. In what amounted to a civil religion sermon, the president in his role as national pastor reassured grief-stricken families and the nation that these men had achieved immortality by sacrificing themselves for 'something immortal'. He offered more than comfort to those who mourned, however. He promised that God had welcomed them into heaven because of their service to the nation. His meaning was unmistakable: 'In giving themselves for others, they made themselves special, not just to us but to their God. . . . We know they live again, not just in our hearts but in His arms. And we know they've gone before to prepare a way for us'. These statements reworked the Christian gospel to such a degree, Pierard and Linder concluded, that at this moment Reagan served 'as the high priest of American civil religion' and did so 'more unabashedly, forcefully, compellingly, and with greater national acceptance than any previous president'. Indeed, he refined the American civil religion to such a degree, they charged, that he brought it into 'direct competition with genuine religion'.[28] This possibility alone is reason enough for believers and non-believers alike to weigh carefully Reagan's interpretation of the American identity and mission.

Working from a large body of Reagan's claims about America from his childhood through his presidency, Pierard and Linder were able to discern at least four distinct yet interrelated beliefs that constituted his civil religion. First, he believed in American exceptionalism, especially the nation's identity as God's chosen people for a special task. Second, he saw America and Americans as inherently good and spiritual, typically speaking of American renewal in terms of a religious awakening. Third, Reagan affirmed that national well-being required what these authors called 'religion-in-general', an indistinct, ecumenical 'faith' that would promote public virtue. And fourth, the president believed that this religious vitality, wedded to military strength, would defeat evil in the world, most notably communist totalitarianism. Using the 'city upon a hill' as a shorthand to sum up Reagan's civil religion, the authors concluded that while, along with millions of Americans, 'the president possessed a personal faith that was genuine and meaningful to him, both he and they subsumed it under the higher public faith'. In the 1980s, they continued, 'civil religion reached a new pinnacle in the American experience as it was exalted by a powerful, priestly president'.[29]

More recently, political scientist Hugh Heclo offered a more conservative critique of Reagan's political theology. He described the Republican president's view of America as something a bit different from, or larger than, exceptionalism. That view, Heclo argued, can best be called 'a sacramental vision'. St. Augustine succinctly defined a sacrament as an outward sign of an inward work of grace. Reagan's metahistory unlocked the inner reality of the American story. For Reagan, Heclo wrote, 'the sacramental quality consisted in understanding the American experience to be set apart as something sacred, a material phenomenon expressing a spiritual reality'. This sacramental reading of America affirmed the nation's 'divine election'; its calling not just to work out its own salvation but to labour on behalf of the world as the 'redeemer nation'; and its role in breaking the cycle of decline and inaugurating a new epoch in human history. Heclo rightly pointed out that long before Reagan Americans had gotten into the habit of saying these kinds of things about their nation. It was only in the more secular late twentieth century that this way of talking started to sound so odd to academics and journalists. Nevertheless, by the end of his largely sympathetic reading of Reagan, Heclo added the caution 'that Reagan was unable to recognize that his faith and redemptive vision of America sailed dangerously close to idolatry, if not quite landing there'. In particular, he faulted Reagan for neglecting Winthrop's more balanced view of what it meant to be a city on a hill, that such visibility meant only that God and man would judge the city, watching to see if it succeeded or failed. Reagan's 'doctrine', Heclo continued, saw 'American goodness with only the barest sense of judgment looming in the background'.[30]

As astute as these two critiques of Reagan's civil theology are, they fail to consider one widely neglected but critical question: whether Reagan, or any American leader for that matter, should ever have called the United States the 'city on a hill' in the first place. Americans need not choose from among an anti-religious secularism that is deaf and blind to theology, or a low-voltage, populist civil religion, or even a more chastened Puritan or Edwardsian sense of national election that keeps a place for divine judgement. The Christians among them can instead reserve divine election and the 'city on a hill' for the Christian Church alone. Christians in the United States can think of themselves from an Augustinian perspective as, first and foremost, citizens of the City of God, living in tension with the world, and sojourning as pilgrims for a time within the current manifestation of the City of Man called 'America'. Keeping their eternal citizenship in mind, they can object when either Democrats or Republicans co-opt any part of the church's identity for their own use, no matter how good their intentions. They can live much of day-to-day life in common with their neighbours, but in the matter of worship, as Augustine wrote in the *City of God*, they must dissent. Part of that dissent means guarding the church's unique identity and calling.

Ronald Reagan took hold of a metaphor and reworked it to such a degree that a nation of 300 million people has lost the ability to hear that metaphor in any way other than how he used it. When Americans today read Winthrop's discourse, their eyes skim over page after page until they find the familiar 'city upon a hill'. When historians and political theorists quote from it and anthologize it, they take care to include the famous passage that readers expect to be there, whether earlier generations thought those were the discourse's defining sections or not. Unless Americans expend great effort, they hear Reagan's voice, not Winthrop's – and certainly not Jesus' – when they encounter the city on a hill. The transmutation of Jesus' message into Winthrop's and then into Kennedy's and Reagan's highlights the complex interplay between the sacred and the secular in modern America, the easy blending of the things of God and the things of Caesar, regardless of how high Americans think the largely imaginary 'wall of separation' stands between politics and religion in their culture.

Newsweek columnist Roger Cohen noted in a review of Godfrey Hodgson's *Myth of American Exceptionalism* in 2009 that from the beginning America has had the 'city upon a hill' imbedded in its 'psyche'. Just how far back that identity really goes is open to historical scrutiny, but he raised a valid point obvious to anyone who spends much time thinking about the American past. 'At the heart of American exceptionalism', he wrote, 'lies a messianic streak, the belief in a country with a global calling to uplift'. After summarizing Hodgson's complaint that Reagan began a trend toward national 'hubris and self-interest' that 'corrupted' a once-noble vision, an otherwise sympathetic Cohen faulted Hodgson for suggesting that a more self-aware 'sobered United States can and should become simply a nation among nations'. The United States' own history made such an ordinary status impossible. 'America was born as an idea', he protested, adding a non sequitur: 'and so it has to carry that idea forward'. Apparently believing that the world needs ideological nations, Cohen worried that the United States 'is in many ways the last ideological country on earth'. 'An American revival', he continued, 'without its universalist embodiment of liberty, democracy, the rule of law and free enterprise seems to me impossible. . . .'[31]

One cannot help but notice how close Cohen, a man of the political Left, sounds to Reagan, crusader for the Right. The words are interchangeable. To be sure, the same words in the mouths of different men can carry very different connotations and meanings. But that truth ought not obscure what the similarity in language reveals about modern American politics and religion. A debate over American exceptionalism is usually a debate between varieties of exceptionalism. Contested meanings for the city on a hill might look and sound like arguments from opposite ends of the ideological spectrum, but in truth they typically consist of left-wing exceptionalists arguing with right-wing exceptionalists – the whole range of emotion from A to B.

A more meaningful and important debate over how to interpret American history and identity might therefore be one between exceptionalists of all sorts on one side and sceptics on the other, that is, between those who believe that the United States is somehow exempt from human finitude, the lust for dominion, and the limits of resources and power, and those who do not. And because exceptionalism has tangled up within it the problem of civil religion, it may well be that the deepest fault line today in American culture lies not along the obvious divide between religious and irreligious people but along the largely overlooked divide between religious orthodoxy and Americanism.

In the 1860s, Fyodor Dostoevsky, through the voice of his Underground Man, predicted that in the age of ideology we would sooner or later figure out how to be born only from an idea and not from real fathers. He may have overestimated the power of ideas, as John Lukacs argues, but he identified a real danger for propositional nations in the modern world. Americans may think that an 'idea' helps them see their national identity more clearly when in fact the very simplicity that makes the American Idea so appealing blinds them to the complexity of their past and inhibits genuine self-understanding. As president, Ronald Reagan guaranteed that for many years – and perhaps forever – the American nation and the city on a hill would be fused into one indistinguishable symbol of universal benevolence. The confusion of kingdoms evident in America's identity as the city on a hill narrows the debate over the American identity to false options. It also renders Christians oblivious to the boundaries between the two cities they inhabit. Such confusion of kingdoms makes the common life that Christians and non-Christians share in this world even more difficult than it already is. Sorting out the confusion requires knowing the difference between the city on a hill and the City of Man.

7

The once and future city

We must remain the Shining City on a Hill to all who seek freedom and prosperity.

SARAH PALIN, 2009

Shortly after the November 2010 mid-term elections, the Public Religion Research Institute surveyed nearly 1,500 voters about 'American values'. Questions covered everything from the economy, to immigration, to health care reform, to gay marriage. When asked if 'God has granted America a special role in human history', 58 per cent agreed. Whether many of these same citizens could articulate just what that destiny meant for the nation is another matter. But this high percentage reveals nevertheless a durable feature of the American identity that has survived world wars, economic depression, terrorist attacks and mounting debt. Regardless of how that 'special role' might translate into domestic or foreign policy, some remnant of the 'redeemer myth' endures in the mainstream culture. It may only superficially resemble John Winthrop's 'special commission', but something of this self-understanding still haunts America's consciousness into the twenty-first century.

Led along an unexpected path, the idea of America as a city on a hill has become one of the most common ways to articulate that sense of divine calling. The burden of this book has been to show how Americans at various stages took Winthrop's city and changed it from a biblical metaphor into a national myth. From time to time, they took the metaphor directly from the Sermon on the Mount to describe their nation, or just their local city, not knowing that it would appear to later generations that they were quoting John Winthrop. They ignored the Model of Christian Charity and continued to do so even after the discourse appeared in print. They did not use it or quote it the way later generations would as a matter of habit. They did not know that one day the Model would be incorporated into the national Scripture alongside the Declaration of Independence and the Gettysburg Address. They did not know it was part of their literary canon. Only in hindsight did Americans adopt the city on a hill as an emblem for who they were as a people. Only belatedly did they embrace it as an affirmation of faith in their evolving civil religion and imagine that they and their ancestors had done so in an unbroken tradition since 1630.

The search for the city on a hill leads to a story of what men and women, some famous, some obscure, did to a metaphor. Only incidentally is it the story of how an idea made Americans into who they were as a people. Ideas are powerful. Ideas do have consequences. But men and women are not the victims of ideas. They take ideas and shape them. At times they are faithful to the meaning of ideas. At other times, they put those ideas to uses alien to their original purpose. Recently, after decades of reflection, John Lukacs has revisited his insight that it is more important and interesting to know what men do to ideas than what ideas do to men. In *The Future of History*, he writes, 'Ideas and beliefs are not abstractions. They are historical, like everything else human. But they are not the obvious outcomes of some kind of *Zeitgeist*'. 'I repeat', he insists: 'recognize that people do not *have* ideas. They choose them.'[1] Americans may find it flattering and inspiring to think that the idea of the city on a hill was imposed on them by God or by history. But the idea did not choose them; they chose it. And in choosing it they turned a biblical metaphor into a national myth with consequences for both Church and State.

Anyone who has studied the Puritans over the past few decades knows that beginning in the 1970s historians worked to recover something closer to the original meaning of the Model of Christian Charity and its celebrated metaphor. Between them and their goal lay the formidable Perry Miller and his influence on a generation of scholars. My concern throughout this book has been to show the ways in which Jesus' and then Winthrop's metaphor was remade into a national myth. Central to that story has been the *unmaking*, however unintentional, of the biblical metaphor at the hands of preachers, politicians and historians. The related story of how historians tried in turn to *unmake* the historical myth that Miller and others perpetuated is a large and important one, but telling that story would quickly take us into a specialized conversation too narrow for this book. I am indebted to the painstaking work of historians who have laboured to move away from the national myth and back to a version of the city on a hill that Winthrop and the Puritans would have acknowledged as closer to what they had in mind in 1630. As a non-specialist in the study of Puritanism, I have learned a great deal from them. Through a slow process, I have come to believe that these historians are largely right about New England's consciousness. Whether they have overcorrected for Miller's image of the Puritans as international revolutionaries is a possibility I leave to others to debate. They have certainly given us a 'city on a hill' much closer to the seventeenth century's understanding of that potent, troubled and tired metaphor, a vantage point from which to see more clearly what has happened to the metaphor in those nearly 400 years.

Most relevant to the search for the city on a hill is what these historians have argued to be true about the content of the metaphor as a mission statement. It has been difficult for students of Puritanism and other authors to shake themselves loose from the habit of mind that takes for granted that this one phrase encapsulates Winthrop's understanding of the Puritan project. The Model of Christian Charity as a whole contains so much more than that phrase can possibly be made to hold. Americans really ought to move beyond this metaphor, perhaps even to the point of ignoring it altogether in favour of the larger context and overall thrust of Winthrop's discourse. Whether we agree with him or not, find his legacy laudatory or pernicious, we do Winthrop an injustice by reducing him to a handy catchphrase. And we miss the chance to learn from the past. Regardless, Winthrop's purpose in choosing the metaphor of the city has undergone significant re-evaluation since Perry Miller. Naturally, these historians have not always agreed with each other and plenty of authors continue to write about the Puritans as if Miller's interpretation of the Puritan mission were definitive. But in the writing of history no one ever gets the last word.

Early on in the response to Miller, Robert Middlekauff argued that Winthrop invoked the image of the city on a hill to call on 'the rest of the world' to 'watch them to see if they held to their professed dedication to purity and Christian love'. 'It seems doubtful', he continued, contra Miller, 'that the hard-headed Winthrop, or any of the Puritans who arrived in the years after 1630, held any hope that the watchers would profit form New England's example'. These were families 'banished' from their homes. They were refugees, 'the Church in exile', he wrote, 'and destined to remain outside the English pale until the end of things'. These were not special ops forces on a mission to remake the world. They were sober realists whose 'obligation was to preserve the Church – not to convert the world, which in any case would resist conversion until the proper point was reached on the line of time'.[2]

This account of the city on a hill might not reckon adequately with the problem, evident near the end of the Model, that the operative metaphor in Winthrop's conclusion was the Hebrews crossing the Jordan into Canaan. Canaan was the Promised Land, after all. Arriving there meant the end of exile. Nevertheless, Middlekauff's sensitive rendering of the city on a hill matches the Winthrop of 1629 who told his wife that he sought 'a shelter and a hiding place for us and others'.[3] In the 1980s, Theodore Dwight Bozeman challenged Miller by name, claiming the Harvard professor had invented the 'idea of an exemplary Puritan mission'. Rather than the Model's interpretive key, the phrase 'city on a hill' was simply a 'rhetorical commonplace'. The discourse as a whole 'was no installment upon an American plan of restless progress' but a call to return to the church's primal purity. The Model anchored itself in the distant past and not an indefinite future, Bozeman wrote.[4] Andrew Delbanco, moreover, found Winthrop more concerned to avoid the shame of becoming the wrong kind of spectacle to the world than with providing a model for global reformation. Winthrop's discourse was 'considerably more focused on what was being fled than on what was being pursued'.[5] And most recently, Winthrop biographer Francis Bremer has emphasized how ordinary the phrase 'city on a hill' was in 1630 and how conventional Winthrop's message likely sounded to his Puritan audience.[6]

One of the ironies in this endeavour, one I find myself falling into, is the tendency to perpetuate the exaggerated historical significance assigned to the city on a hill in the very act of trying to recover its historical *insignificance*. By trying to put it back in its place we risk drawing even more attention to it. But if that is true, it is a problem created by those who distorted the metaphor in the first place. As a historian interested in the complex interplay between people and ideas, I share these scholars' concern to understand the Model of Christian Charity on its own terms. My efforts are imperfect and like all historical accounts, provisional. When I go back to the Model of Christian Charity, I do not find hidden in the metaphor of the city, a prophecy about the United States. I do not see a national mission statement in these few words. Nor do I see the point of origin for America's political institutions, for democracy, or individualism, or free enterprise. I do not see any normative precedent for open or closed borders, for a strong national defense, a robust economy, or 'energy independence'. These are all legitimate matters of concern for statesmen charged with the stewardship of a nation's resources and the shaping of public policy. They touch on vital aspects of domestic and foreign affairs that affect every American and people around the world. But

Winthrop's concerns were not our concerns. He did not have our world in mind when he wrote.

Nevertheless, Winthrop's words are often taken as an imperative, as if they were his marching orders to his fellow Puritan colonists to *build* the city on a hill. Elsewhere in his long discourse, the governor certainly did plead with the colonists to cultivate brotherly affection, to work hard to create an enduring commonwealth founded on Christian love. But the city on a hill, as we have seen, was not a goal to work toward. It was for Winthrop an inescapable condition of who these people already were and what they were called to achieve in the New World. Winthrop told them not that they should *build* a city on a hill but rather that 'we *shall be* as a city upon a hill'. And that was an announcement, not a prediction. Their identity as a city was not theirs to choose once they had entered into a special covenant with God, once they had taken the fateful, ominous step of engaging that divine commission. They would be a city by the very nature of who they were and what they were busy doing. Like King Saul, they would either live up to the demands of that commission or their kingdom would be taken from them. As a city on a hill, they had to get it right, obey God, fulfill his commission or lose their kingdom. They did not need to strive to *become* a city a hill. They would *be* that city. Their urgent calling was to labour obediently to honour God's name and not become a byword and a shipwreck. They would either be a spectacle to the world of covenantal blessing or a spectacle to the world of shame and divine chastisement. The eyes of the world would be upon them in either case. They would be a city on a hill regardless. Unlike Hawthorne's Hollingsworth, they did not need to make themselves into a spectacle to the world. It came with the job. In the seventeenth and eighteenth century, the words of Matthew 5.14 were sometimes rendered as 'a city built upon a hill'. But that possibility would not have changed Winthrop's point in the slightest. A conspicuous city was what the community was, not what it aspired to be. Those aspirations were handled in considerable detail elsewhere in the discourse.

In this sense, America has undoubtedly been a city on a hill over the past four centuries. Apart from any striving or building, America has been a spectacle to the world. Since at least the eighteenth century, first as a cluster of British colonies and then as an independent republic and ultimately as a global superpower, America has been subjected to a degree of scrutiny beyond that experienced by any other nation or people. French, English, Dutch, Swiss and German spectators, armchair philosophers, curious novelists and intrepid adventurers, have all pondered the meaning of America, whether they saw the land and her people as the hope of humanity or a menace to civilization. The eyes of the world have indeed been upon America. Whatever Americans' own intentions have been, whatever institutions they might have envisioned creating, whatever they might have intended to exemplify to the rest of the world, they have been on display. If Winthrop had been graced with prophetic foresight, if the 'city on a hill' somehow really was a prediction about the United States, then he hit this part of the prophecy with perfect aim.

The contentious issue is not whether America has been a spectacle to the world. That it has been and continues to be is clear enough. Its vast economic, military and cultural power alone is enough to guarantee that status. What is contested is the kind of city Americans were supposed to inhabit, just what ideas and institutions that city would model for the world. The relevance of all this for the context of twenty-first-century America is that the nation's political culture, Left and Right, presupposes that Winthrop called on the Puritans to *build* a city on a hill and by extension prophetically summoned the United States to that same task. Democrats and Republicans might give that mission statement different content, but both parties accept the mission. They might envision different secular, political agendas for the never-quite-finished city under perpetual construction, but they agree that the city on a hill needs to be built.

The American Left's efforts today to maintain a liberal version of the city on a hill seem timid. This lackluster attempt is true despite the fact that they have such clear title to the metaphor. They invented its modern use. It appeared in modern politics thanks to their icon John F. Kennedy. Throughout the 1980s, Democratic leaders responded to Reagan at key intervals to reassert a social-justice version of the city based on Winthrop's use of Micah 6.8 ('What does the Lord require of you but to do justice, love mercy and to walk humbly with your God?'). In 1997, President Bill Clinton used the Model of Christian Charity to extol the 'great American experiment' not as the city on a hill but as a social compact. 'Winthrop told his shipmates', the president said, placing the scene below deck for some reason, '. . . that in America we must be knit together in this work as one man – rejoice together, mourn together, labor and suffer together, always having before our eyes our community in the work, our community as members of one body'. It is interesting to see the political uses to which the 'one body' of the Church of Jesus could be put.

But as Reagan became an increasingly revered figure in American memory, even among liberals, the Democrats seemed less and less willing to challenge his shining city. In June 2004, a few weeks after Reagan's death, Democratic presidential candidate John Kerry praised Reagan in several campaign stops, pausing only to remind an audience of supporters in San Jose, California, of his own ancestral claim to the city on a hill. The Massachusetts Senator's maternal grandmother was in fact a Winthrop, a reminder of how durable the Boston elite has been in American politics. More recently, Kathleen Kennedy Townsend, Robert Kennedy's daughter, ventured in the *Atlantic* to criticize Reagan for never offering 'any detailed description of how to actually build the city'. His vision was constrained and debased by 'anti-government rhetoric' that conceived of Americans only as so many disconnected individuals chasing after personal fulfillment in hot pursuit of selfish material gain. She called instead for a vision closer to her father's, a national ethic that reaffirmed widespread participation in 'building the city', one that pursued an older notion of human flourishing and the common good through 'a fair and just society'.[7] This alternative did indeed echo RFK's 1965 call for America to

finish its journey toward social justice. But beyond such occasional affirmations of the more communitarian side of the city on a hill, Democrats seemed
unlikely to challenge Reagan in their campaigns. A direct attack would too
easily appear to be a direct assault on the man himself rather than on a set of
policies, as Mario Cuomo sensed in 1984.

The Left's liability is, of course, the Right's asset. And conservatives,
especially neoconservatives, have shown that they know what to do with the
Reagan legacy. They deploy the city on a hill aggressively. It serves them as
a shorthand not simply for America or conservative values, but for the kind
of America associated with Reagan—or at least what Republican voters have
popularly associated with the Reagan years: minimal government bureau-
cracy, lower taxes, a strong national defense and a dose of 'Morning in
America' optimism. Neoconservative journalists and think-tank analysts,
savvy Republican candidates and officeholders, and a few evangelicals allied
with them try to keep the city on a hill shining brightly.

Bestselling historian Robert Kagan, a senior fellow at the Brookings
Institution, columnist for the *Washington Post*, contributing editor for the
neoconservative *Weekly Standard*, and founder with William Kristol of the
Project for the New American Century, has argued that the city on a hill has
symbolized anything but an isolationist tradition in US foreign policy. In
his 2006 survey of America's role in the world, *Dangerous Nation*, he called
the Puritans of New England the 'first imperialists'. He rejected the 'myth'
of a merely exemplary, idealist America to advance an interpretation of the
Puritans as aggressively expansionist 'global revolutionaries'. He resurrected
Perry Miller's 'Calvinist internationale' – without the nuances. Indeed, Kagan
relied almost exclusively on Miller to characterize the Puritan project in the
New World and from them to set the trajectory of the American mission.[8]

Aiming at a more popular audience, David Gelernter offered another robust
version of the city on hill in his extraordinary 2007 book, *Americanism*. A
professor at Yale and a contributing editor of *The Weekly Standard*, Gelernter

made Winthrop and the Puritans the centerpiece of his nationalist manifesto for a political theology. He celebrated the United States as a modern 'biblical republic' and 'Americanism' as a world religion complete with a universal creed. The origin of that faith in America as the 'light of the world' was none other than the Bible-wielding Puritans – a new chosen people entering a new Promised Land. There they built the city on a hill, the beginnings of America's 'sacred mission' to spread 'liberty, equality, and democracy'. 'John Winthrop was a founder of this nation, we are his heirs, and thank God we have inherited his humanitarian decency along with his radical God-fearing Americanism'.[9] Winthrop reinvented as an acolyte of a new religion called 'Americanism' shows the extent to which some still labour to sustain the city on a hill as a national myth.

In the run-up to the 2008 Republican primaries and presidential campaign, candidates appealed to the city on a hill more frequently than ever before in American history. New York mayor Rudy Giuliani and former Massachusetts governor Mitt Romney invoked it. John McCain tossed it to the crowd at the New Hampshire primary. But out-distancing them all was Alaska governor Sarah Palin. From almost the moment of her nomination, the Republican vice presidential candidate mentioned Reagan and his shining city in stop after stop on the campaign trail. In Palin's hands, the metaphor took on perhaps its most intensely populist and nationalist colouring to date. In *Going Rogue*, her 2009 autobiography, she called for a 'commonsense conservatism' of economic development and a strong national defense. Toward the end of the book, in her only reference to the metaphor, she denied that America was a predatory empire out to 'force our ideals' on other nations. Nevertheless, the American people 'have been given a unique responsibility: to show the world the meaning and the rewards of freedom. America, as Reagan said, is "the abiding alternative to tyranny". We must remain the Shining City on a Hill to all who seek freedom and prosperity'.[10]

America By Heart, Palin's next book, followed a year later.[11] Here she openly identified herself with 'Tea Party Americans' and acknowledged their fears as her own. She used Reagan's version of the metaphor far more frequently here than in her previous book, this time linking it to the contentious issue of American exceptionalism. So effective have this and other efforts been to fuse these two ideas that for many Republicans the city on a hill is now interchangeable with exceptionalism. The metaphor's latest job description is to serve as a slogan for exceptionalism. Palin used either 'exceptional' or 'exceptionalism' more than 30 times to describe America in this book. She contrasted Reagan's affirmation of faith in the shining city with what she saw as President Barack Obama's embarrassment over the nation's unique calling and destiny. 'And we're worried', she wrote of herself and the Tea Party, 'that our leaders don't believe what we believe: that America is an exceptional nation, the shining city on a hill that Ronald Reagan believed it is'.[12]

Combined in this way, exceptionalism and the city on a hill became a means for Palin, as for the neoconservative journalists and media pundits she quoted from, to tell a new version of the American narrative. This template allowed her and them to build a single story reaching from John Winthrop to Alexis de Tocqueville to Abraham Lincoln, to John F. Kennedy to Ronald Reagan. All it required to be chosen for this lineage was some affirmation of America's special destiny. That minimal requirement has become the principle of selection and organization of American history. And there in the middle of it all sits the city on a hill. A telling example of this strategy appeared in Palin's third chapter: 'America the Exceptional'. It is worth quoting at length. After praising a 2010 article in *National Review* defending exceptionalism, the former governor wrote:

The idea of American exceptionalism is older than the United States itself. When Ronald Reagan used to speak of a "shining city on a hill", he was borrowing from John Winthrop, a preacher who led a group of Puritans to religious freedom in America in 1630.

"We shall be as a city upon a hill. The eyes of all people are upon us."

Winthrop, in turn, was borrowing from Matthew 5:14, in which Jesus tells his followers, "You are the light of the world. A city that is set on a hill cannot be hidden."

"The light of the world." "A city on a hill." These are high aspirations for a people in a strange new land.[13]

High aspirations indeed. Palin soon arrived at Jack Kennedy, praising his Inaugural Address for its stirring affirmation 'of America as a place with a meaning and a mission of redemption'.[14] This was certainly true of Kennedy, his brother Robert and much of the Democratic left in the 1960s. But the remarkable thing here is how nonchalantly the high-profile conservative Palin embraced this liberal heritage in her effort to place President Obama outside the American narrative. As part of that strategy, the image of the city on a hill enabled her to amalgamate anything into the latest version of the one story of what America is and was always meant to be. The complex differences between Winthrop, Kennedy and Reagan magically vanished.

One further tendency in Palin's use of exceptionalism is worth mentioning. She exemplifies how the historic Christian teaching about the church's mission in the world can be simultaneously nationalized and individualized. Describing the moment as a child when she committed her life to God's service, she recounted her epiphany at a camp in the Alaska wilderness that 'surely God has a purpose for all of us – and He expects a lot from us!' A few pages later she returned to that moment at camp and then added the parallel insight: 'I believe my country, too, has a purpose: to be a shining city on a hill, a beacon of liberty and hope for all the peoples of the earth'.[15] Overshadowed by this heartfelt piety and patriotism is any notion of the church as the city on a hill.

Palin's populist, nationalist message seemed to resonate with many American voters disaffected with mainstream Republican politics, but by 2011 she had not yet translated her version of the city on a hill into national electoral victory. Florida Republican Marco Rubio did just that. In his maiden speech on the floor of the Senate in June 2011, the freshman Senator managed to combine John F. Kennedy's 'watchman on the walls of world freedom' and Henry Luce's 'American century' with robust exceptionalism and Reagan's shining city. At the end of his speech, he rejected the idea that America had reached the limit of its wealth, power and influence and was about to be surpassed by 'new shining cities'. He accepted the costs, he vowed, of 'keep[ing] America's light shining' and envisioned multiple shining cities encircling the globe. 'America never wanted to be the only shining city on the hill', he claimed. 'We wanted our example to inspire the people of the earth to build one of their own'. American influence would not be diminished in the company of such exemplary cities following America's lead. Indeed, the light of these other exemplary nations 'is but a reflection of our own'. And that light was nothing less than 'the light of an American century that now spreads throughout the earth'.[16]

None of these defenses of America as the city on a hill coming from the ranks of Republicans and neoconservatives sounded odd to millions of evangelicals who believed in America's unique heritage and identity as a Christian nation. Nothing seemed strange about an America dressed in biblical imagery to a generation of Christians taught to read their nation's history as a manifestation of the special relationship between their land and their God. Since the 1970s, such bestselling books as *The Light and the Glory* and its sequels had turned the events of American history into proof of the finger of God in history. Winthrop's Model of Christian Charity, with its evocation of love as the basis of a godly community, fit securely in that deeply providential story. The meaning of Winthrop's enterprise could not have been clearer to the co-authors. From the stones 'in the rocky fields of New England', the Puritans had laid 'the foundation stones, not merely of American democracy, but of the Kingdom of God in America'.[17]

More recently, the *American Patriot's Bible* has shown the lengths to which the amalgamation of nationalism and Christianity can go. Released by Thomas Nelson, one of the world's oldest Bible publishers, it combines features of a traditional family Bible (pages to record births, marriages and deaths) with inspiring bits of Americana. It juxtaposes an angel lifting a cross, with the Marines on the Iwo Jima Memorial lifting the flag. The point in words and pictures is to show how Scripture made America unique and great and how a return to those biblical roots will secure the nation's future as a righteous people. The results defy description. The sacred and the secular have never been more seamlessly integrated. Patriot stands with Patriarch, Decalogue with Declaration, Noah with Noah Webster. It is all one story. Even a rugged 'camo' edition is available for soldiers – covered in 'the official MultiCam® fabric used on the US Military's uniforms and packs', the publisher's website promises. Next to Matthew 5.14, the editors placed not the expected passage from John Winthrop but Peter Bulkeley's *Gospel Covenant* as the authoritative gloss on Jesus' metaphor. Twice elsewhere the notes mention Winthrop as Reagan's source for the 'shining city'. And in the introduction to the Old Testament book of Micah, the explanatory notes cite the Model of Christian Charity's use of Micah 6.8. A box next to the verse explains that this is where 'Jimmy Carter placed his hand . . . as he took the presidential oath of office in 1977'. If nothing else, the *American Patriot's Bible* ought to remind us that American Christians have not been innocent victims while the nation co-opted their language and symbols, not in the 1860s and not today. Their faith in this instance was not diluted by some mysterious 'secularization'. They did the job themselves.

Today, 50 years after the city on a hill first appeared in modern political rhetoric and nearly 400 years since John Winthrop shepherded his flock to New England's shores, Americans are left with a secularized metaphor, politicized by the Left and the Right and nearing the point of exhaustion. The metaphor has been forced to carry an impossible load of nationalist, populist and collectivist aspirations. Americans have inherited two political cities looming so large in the media, the political culture and even the church, that together they have eclipsed the historical Winthrop and the biblical Jesus. The biblical metaphor, appropriated by the Puritans and reinvented by modern Democrats and Republicans, has been transformed so successfully into a national myth that few can see or hear these words without all of their modern political meaning attached. Even many Christians, who might be expected to guard their property more vigilantly, argue over which national values the politicized city should stand for and miss the fact that they have lost their metaphor. They argue over which party ought to build the city, over whether Kennedy's or Reagan's vision best defines the city, rarely stopping to consider whether Jesus ever had America in mind in the Sermon on the Mount. Such is the power of civil religion in twenty-first century America. Even if Americans manage to convince themselves, in spite of the evidence, that John Winthrop envisioned a glorious future for American ideals and institutions, can they really convince themselves that Jesus intended the United States to take up his disciples' calling as a city on a hill? Distracted by a contest between two earthly political cities, Americans forget that the original city on a hill was neither Democrat or Republican. It was not even American.

Liberals are probably right that the communitarian ethic associated with the modern welfare state adheres more closely to Winthrop's vision for New England than the libertarian individualism of the minimalist state does. But even if that affinity between the Puritans and modern liberalism turned out to be the case, making sure America 'gets right with Winthrop' in a revival of national faith is not the point of the city on a hill. Winthrop's political and economic theories are not necessarily appropriate for modern America. Americans make Winthrop and his Model into the blueprint for their activism because somehow that legitimizes their policies as authentically American. Adding a line or two from the Model of Christian Charity might lend a superficial authority to their agenda. But all they really end up doing is reinventing Winthrop into a rough draft of themselves. Handled in this way, the past can be turned into a precedent for anything and everything. What gets lost is the problem that Jesus' city on a hill was never the American, or any nation's, mission in the first place.

The Puritans, John Winthrop, the Model of Christian Charity, and the city on a hill have important things to teach Americans and the rest of the world about the history of the United States. But they are not the whole story of what America was and has become. Any attempt to squeeze 400 years into one movement, or leader, or document, or slogan can only obscure the vast complexity of the nation's history. Such radical simplification distorts the past. It turns it into raw materials to be re-shaped and mobilized into any modern cause or campaign. The Model of Christian Charity mattered and still matters as part of the American identity, but it does not matter to the degree most Americans have assumed for the past half century. At one time, Winthrop's discourse did not define the meaning and purpose of the United States at all. What Americans have come to assume Winthrop meant by the 'city on a hill' is really what the present generation has chosen to believe about a mythic American past they are striving to return to or an elusive mythic future they are striving to reach. Metaphors are unavoidable. They help us to explain the unknown in terms of the known. We probably cannot think or speak without them. But that possibility does not mean we do not have to be on our guard when using them. They can reveal similarities we would otherwise miss. But they can also obscure important differences. In the case of the city on a hill, continued use of the metaphor eclipses fundamental distinctions between the America that was and the America that is and between the things of God and the things of Caesar.

But is there a healthier alternative? Could the metaphor of the city on a hill serve another, more constructive purpose for America? It is indeed possible to imagine Jesus' metaphor recovering more specific historic and intellectual content, of it serving as a reminder to Americans to watch their 'doctrine and life', as a modern Jonathan Edwards might urge them to, and to live together under a sense of divine judgement. In this way, some might say, the city on a hill could help bind the nation together and help hold public officials to high standards of character and conduct. Defined by some creedal content, the city on a hill might help the nation live up to the best of its inherited institutions and principles.

A city on a hill that underwent this sort of urban-renewal effort might benefit America. But it would do nothing for Christians who have lost their metaphor. Nothing to address the problem of America thinking of itself as some version of the Kingdom of God on Earth. Even if the metaphor had not been secularized and had been allowed to retain a meaning closer to its original purpose, something closer, that is, to the exegetical consensus of the church we explored in Chapter 2, there still would be a problem. Any nation that promoted itself as the earthly embodiment of the community of brotherly affection and mutual self-sacrifice that Winthrop drew from the New Testament's description of the church would become to some degree a replacement for the church. It would become a new religion, much as Gelernter hoped America would. But a nation-state cannot take on the calling of the apostles or the Body of Christ without damaging both church and state. The language of the church cannot be appropriated by the state without conse-quences. The long tradition of Christian political theology has maintained, despite considerable internal debate and important exceptions, that the confusion between the 'things of Caesar' and the 'things of God' threatens the integrity of both realms. It elevates the secular government beyond its calling and capacity and robs the church of an essential part of its identity.

Wrapped in the American flag, the biblical metaphor of the city on a hill loses its power to identify the church. If Americans, even Christians, think first of the United States when they hear those words, then the political use of the metaphor has imposed a cost that modern disciples of Jesus ought to consider. The light of the gospel and the teaching ministry of the church have been remade into affirmations of American optimism, social justice, economic prosperity and exceptionalism. The 'good news' has been overshadowed by a feel-good political agenda. By now, the 'city on a hill' is so closely identified with the United States that the metaphor has been destroyed for American Christians. They have lost control and ownership of their metaphor. Jesus gave this metaphor to his disciples just as he gave them the metaphor of salt and light. But Christians in America fail to notice or care when their nation appropriates their God-given identity for its own purposes. Do they assume that America's purposes and the church's purposes are the same? Is America indeed the functional equivalent of the universal church for otherwise autonomous Christians, as some scholars have suggested? If George W. Bush's use of the Gospel of John in 2002 could have been such a non-event, then should it be any wonder that the ubiquitous political use of 'city on a hill' has rendered this metaphor invisible and inaudible to Christians?

For the political appropriation of biblical imagery to become visible and audible it would be necessary for the 'city on a hill' to become a problem. The distinguished British historian R. A. Markus once wrote that the Roman Empire became a problem for Augustine in the fifth century in the wake of the Goths' sack of the Eternal City.[18] Under the influence of the North African bishop's teaching, Christians who had once embraced Rome's messianic identity as a Christianized empire called to redeem the world eventually rejected that view in favour of Augustine's tempered view of Rome as, yes, used by God in history to fulfill His inscrutable purposes, but not as God's New Israel. Rome was simply the most recent manifestation of the City of Man. If it was possible for fifth-century Christians to recognize Rome's earthly, temporal identity, then it ought to be possible for a new generation of Christians to recognize the United States as the City of Man. Christians owe a proper degree of allegiance to their nation. Christians ought to love their earthly home with well-ordered affections. But they must be on guard against idolatry in whatever form it takes. They must not give to Caesar anything that belongs to Christ and his Church no matter how much they love their country. In fact, a proper love of their country will keep them from ascribing any untruth to the thing they love. In Christian theology, it is simply not true that America is the city on a hill, not now, not ever. To seek to protect America from this falsehood is not to do her any dishonour. Quite the opposite. It spares her from delusion. Proper love refuses to cooperate with the effort to divinize America. We would not indulge any friend's fantasy that he is the Messiah. We would get him the help he needs. Compassionately, we would try to guide our friend out of that delusion and into good mental health. Likewise, it would be healthy for America to see itself – and if that goal is too ambitious, then for Christians in America to see their nation – as part of the kingdom of this world, called in the Providence of God to fulfill its earthly purpose but not called to be the Saviour of the World.

Prospects for Christians recovering their metaphor seem dim. Such a recovery is unlikely in the foreseeable future – as unlikely as recovering the 'house divided' from its association with Lincoln and the Civil War. There is no guarantee that 'city on a hill' can be rid of its identification with the United States and returned to the church. Some dramatic event or sly parody in film or television in the future might be powerful enough to eclipse Reagan's 'city on a hill' and even Winthrop's in American memory. Such a possibility seems hard to imagine while Reagan's influence remains so strong. But it is conceivable. Would that new version of the city on a hill be another political remaking of the metaphor? Would that new version be a snide postmodern joke that emptied it of all meaning whatsoever? The church certainly cannot force Caesar to give back its metaphor. Caesar has gotten good service out of it. He still finds it useful. But there is no reason why Christians have to cooperate with Caesar's appropriation of the city on a hill. The more self-conscious Americans in general become about using the metaphor, and the better they know the story of how the city was turned from a biblical metaphor into a national myth, the more likely they are to abandon it as a tired emblem of their collective aspirations as a people. If this is so, then it presents an opportunity for Christians to 'take back' the metaphor, not for Reagan or the Republican Party, not for social justice or another liberal cause, but for the church to which it originally and exclusively belonged.

A Note on Sources

Anyone interested in exploring the Puritans, John Winthrop, Jonathan Edwards, and America's political theology further will find the following books useful. From the earliest stages of planning for this book, I intended to satisfy my own curiosity and to help answer the questions of professional historians and other scholars who, like me, wondered how America became the 'city on a hill'. But I also wanted to help general readers understand the nuances of the American civil religion, the contours of historical thinking, and exactly how John Winthrop's Model of Christian Charity and its famous phrase got woven into the narrative of the nation's identity. The endnotes accompanying the text will guide readers to my primary and secondary sources, but a few are worth highlighting for those who seek further understanding of these problems. This list makes no attempt to be comprehensive and could be multiplied tenfold.

Edmund S. Morgan's *The Puritan Dilemma* (Boston: Little, Brown, 1958) offers an astute, brief account of John Winthrop and the Puritan project in the New World. On the history of early New England more generally, see Robert Middlekauff, *The Mathers: Three Generations of Puritan Intellectuals, 1596–1728* (New York: Oxford University Press, 1971); Francis J. Bremer, *The Puritan Experiment: New England Society from Bradford to Edwards* (New York: St. Martin's Press, 1976); Sacvan Bercovitch's controversial but influential two studies, *The Puritan Origins of the American Self* (New Haven: Yale University Press, 1975) and *The American Jeremiad* (Madison: University of Wisconsin Press, 1978); Theodore Dwight Bozeman, *To Live Ancient Lives: The Primitivist Dimension in Puritanism* (Chapel Hill: University of

North Carolina Press, 1988); and Andrew Delbanco, *The Puritan Ordeal* (Cambridge: Harvard University Press, 1989). The most recent and comprehensive Winthrop biography is Francis J. Bremer, *John Winthrop: America's Forgotten Founding Father* (New York: Oxford University Press, 2003). For fresh, provocative insights into what became known as the Puritan Migration, see Susan Hardman Moore, *Pilgrims: New World Settlers and the Call of Home* (New Haven: Yale University Press, 2007). Moore directly and indirectly challenges many assumptions at the heart of American exceptionalism. Additionally, the works of Samuel Eliot Morison and Perry Miller, despite good reasons for caution, remain integral to the ongoing debate about the Puritans in America and provide the necessary backdrop for understanding the revisions offered by later historians.

The standard biography of New England's leading eighteenth-century theologian is George M. Marsden, *Jonathan Edwards: A Life* (New Haven: Yale University Press, 2003). Marsden's work on Edwards offers a model of scholarship and historical consciousness. For an analysis of how Edwards related his theology to civil society, see Gerald R. McDermott, *One Holy and Happy Society: The Public Theology of Jonathan Edwards* (University Park: Pennsylvania State University Press, 1992). Yale's decades-long project to bring Edwards' sermons, treatises and letters into print and onto the Web continues to expand access to these indispensable resources for students of American religion.

The nineteenth-century clash over how to tell the American story remains wide open as a field for further historical inquiry. Groundbreaking work has been done by Anne Norton, *Alternative Americas: A Reading of Antebellum Political Culture* (Chicago: University of Chicago Press, 1986); Harlow Sheidley, *Sectional Nationalism: Massachusetts Conservative Leaders and the Transformation of America, 1815–1836* (Boston: Northeastern University Press, 1998); and Susan-Mary Grant, *North Over South: Northern Nationalism and American Identity in the Antebellum Era* (Lawrence: University Press of Kansas, 200). The standard biographies of historian George Bancroft are Russell B. Nye, *George Bancroft: Brahmin Rebel* (New York: Alfred A. Knopf, 1945) and Lilian Handlin, *George Bancroft: The Intellectual as Democrat* (New York: Harper & Row, 1984). Any scholar with the courage and tenacity to go through vast collections of largely unprocessed and/or uncatalogued papers would find more than enough material for a fresh treatment of this nearly forgotten man of letters.

For America's civil religion, the starting point is still the classic study by Lee Tuveson, *Redeemer Nation: The Idea of America's Millennial Role* (Chicago: University of Chicago Press, 1968). The literature on this subject is vast and growing, but a few notable books include Nicholas Guyatt, *Providence and the Invention of the United States, 1607–1876* (Cambridge: Cambridge University Press, 2007); Jan Willem Schulte Nordholt, *The Myth of the West: America as the Last Empire* (Grand Rapids: Eerdmans, 1995); Conrad Cherry's anthology *God's New Israel: Religious Interpretations of American Destiny* (Chapel Hill: UNC Press, 1998); and Darryl Hart, *A Secular Faith: Why Christianity Favors the Separation of Church and State* (Chicago: Ivan R. Dee, 2006). On the Model of Christian Charity in the context of American religious history, see Larry Witham, *A City Upon a Hill: How Sermons Changed the Course of American History* (New York: HarperOne, 2007). One of the most ambitious attempts to read the Model as a political treatise is Matthew S. Holland, *Bonds of Affection: Civic Charity and the Making of America – Winthrop, Jefferson, and Lincoln* (Washington, DC: Georgetown University Press, 2007).

Recent critiques of American exceptionalism can be found in Godfrey Hodgson, *The Myth of American Exceptionalism* (New Haven: Yale Unviersity Press, 2009) and Andrew J. Bacevich, *The Limits of Power: The End of American Exceptionalism* (New York: Metropolitan Books, 2008). For a broader treatment, see Seymour Martin Lipset, *American Exceptionalism: A Double-Edged Sword* (New York: W. W. Norton, 1996) and Deborah L. Madsen, *American Exceptionalism* (Jackson: University Press of Mississippi, 1998).

NOTES

Introduction

1 Recent examples include 'City on a Hill' charter schools; a critically acclaimed stage play called 'Shining City'; a reference to Manhattan as the 'city on a hill' on AMC's Emmy-winning drama 'Mad Men'; and the gated Christian community called 'City on a Hill' in the 2011 satirical film *Salvation Boulevard*.

2 Michael McGiffert, 'God's Controversy with Jacobean England', *The American Historical Review*, Vol. 88, No. 5 (December 1983) 1157.

3 Herbert Butterfield, *The Whig Interpretation of History* (New York: W. W. Norton, 1965) 43.

4 John Lukacs, *Historical Consciousness: The Remembered Past*, with a new introduction by the author and a foreword by Russell Kirk (New Brunswick, NJ: Transaction, 1994) 126. See also p. 148.

5 Ernest Lee Tuveson, *Redeemer Nation: The Idea of America's Millennial Role* (Chicago: University of Chicago Press, 1968).

6 Andrew Delbanco, *The Puritan Ordeal* (Cambridge: Harvard University Press, 1989) 72.

7 Richard M. Gamble, *The War for Righteousness: The Progressive Clergy, the Great War, and the Rise of the Messianic Nation* (Wilmington, DE: ISI Books, 2003).

Chapter One

1 George Brown Tindall and David Emory Shi, *America: A Narrative History*, Brief 7th edn. (New York: W. W. Norton, 2007) 35.

2 Cotton's chosen text was 2 Samuel 7.10: 'Moreover I will appoint a place for my people Israel, and I will plant them, that they may dwell in a place of their own, and move no more'. Quotations taken from John Cotton, *God's Promise to His Plantations* (1630) reprinted in *Old South Leaflets*, No. 53.

3 John Cotton to a Minister in England, 3 December 1634, in *The Correspondence of John Cotton*, Sargent Bush, Jr. ed. (Chapel Hill: University of North Carolina Press, 2001) 184. I have modernized the spelling.

4 John Winthrop, 'General Observations for the Plantation of New England', in *Winthrop Papers*, Vol. II (Boston: Massachusetts Historical Society, 1931) 111.

5   John Winthrop to Margaret Winthrop, 15 May 1629, *Winthrop Papers*, II: 91–2.

6   Susan Hardman Moore, *Pilgrims: New World Settlers and the Call of Home* (New Haven: Yale University Press, 2007) 1, 55, 81.

7   Robert Ryece to John Winthrop, 12 August 1629, in *Winthrop Papers*, II: 105–6.

8   Winthrop's journal has appeared in several editions since 1790. The most complete and best-annotated edition is *The Journal of John Winthrop, 1630–1649*, edited by Richard S. Dunn, James Savage, and Laetitia Yeandle (Cambridge: Belknap Press of Harvard University Press, 1996).

9   *Proceedings of the Massachusetts Historical Society*, Vol. XVIII, 1880–1881 (Boston: Massachusetts Historical Society, 1881) 300.

10 Listed as 'BV Winthrop, John' in collections of the New-York Historical Society and used by the Society's permission. I have compared this manuscript against the transcription in the *Winthrop Papers*, II:282–95. In most cases, I have modernized the spelling, punctuation, and capitalization of sixteenth- and seventeenth-century documents to minimize the confusion they can cause for modern readers. While these changes sacrifice something of the texture of colonial America, the sheer complexity of the wording of these documents can distract us from their logic and flow.

11 Hugh J. Dawson, 'John Winthrop's Rite of Passage: The Origins of the "Christian Charitie" Discourse', *Early American Literature*, 26 (1991) 219–31.

12 *Journal*, 314, 590.

13 Quotations taken from the version of the Model published in Volume II of the *Winthrop Papers*, pp. 282–95, and compared against the manuscript copy at the New-York Historical Society. I have modernized spelling and punctuation.

14 See Matthew 22.21. Jesus responded to a question about whether it was right to pay taxes to the Roman government by saying, 'Render to Caesar the things that are Caesar's, and to God the things that are God's'.

Chapter Two

1   For these and other examples, see the volume on Matthew 1–13 in Manlio Simonetti ed., *Ancient Christian Commentary on Scripture* (Downers Grove, IL: InterVarsity, 2001) 91–5; Chrysostom, *The Homilies of S. John Chrysostom, Archbishop of Constantinople, On the Gospel of St. Matthew*, Part I, Hom. I–XXV (Oxford: John Henry Parker, 1843) 212–13; and Thomas Aquinas, *Commentary On the Four Gospels Collected Out of the Works of the Fathers*, Vol. I (Oxford: John Henry Parker, 1841) 162.

2   Martin Luther, *Luther's Works*, Vol. 21, Jaroslav Pelikan ed. (St. Louis, MO: Concordia, 1956) 61–4.

3 John Calvin, *A Harmony of the Gospels, Matthew, Mark, and Luke*, Vol. I, translated by A. W. Morrison, in David W. Torrance and Thomas F. Torrance (eds), *Calvin's Commentaries* (Grand Rapids, MI: Eerdmans, 1972) 177.

4 Darryl Hart, *A Secular Faith: Why Christianity Favors the Separation of Church and State* (Chicago: Ivan R. Dee, 2006) 36–7.

5 These annotations on Matthew 5.14 were collected in the sixteenth century by Augustine Marlorate in *A Catholicke and Ecclesiasticall Exposition of the Holy Gospell after S. Mathewe . . .*, Thomas Tymme (trans.) (London, 1570) 85–7.

6 William Perkins, *A Godly and Learned Exposition Upon Christs Sermon in the Mount* (London: Printed by John Haviland for James Boler, 1631) 26–7. Cambridge University Press published several earlier editions of this work.

7 John Diodati, Annotations Upon S. Matthew, in *Pious and Learned Annotations Upon the Holy Bible: Plainly Expounding the Most Difficult Places Thereof*, 2d edn. (London: Printed by Miles Flesher for Nicholas Fussell, 1648) 8.

8 See Richard T. Hughes, *Myths America Lives By*, Foreword by Robert N. Bellah (Urbana: University of Illinois Press, 2003); William Haller, *Elect Nation: The Meaning and Relevance of Foxe's Book of Martyrs* (New York: Harper & Row, 1963); and Nicholas Guyatt, *Providence and the Invention of the United States, 1607–1876* (Cambridge: Cambridge University Press, 2007).

9 *Journal of John Winthrop*, 324–5.

10 Reprinted in Robert C. Winthrop, *Life and Letters of John Winthrop*, Vol. II (Boston: Ticknor and Fields, 1867) 422–7.

11 Robert Cushman, 'Reasons and Considerations Touching the Lawfulness of Removing Out of England Into the Parts of America', in William Bradford, *A Relation or Journal of the Beginning and Proceedings of the English Plantation Settled at Plymouth in New England . . .* (London: Printed for John Bellamie, 1622) 66.

Chapter Three

1 Francis J. Bremer, *John Winthrop: America's Forgotten Founding Father* (Oxford: Oxford University Press, 2003) 181. Bremer gives the context as the reign of Elizabeth, but the original reference is to the reign of her half-sister, Mary Tudor.

2 Roger Hayden ed., *The Records of a Church of Christ in Bristol, 1640–1687* (Bristol: Bristol Record Society, 1974) 86. In the 1640s, the Bristol congregation took refuge with Henry Jessey's congregation in London. This was the same Jessey who asked John Winthrop, Jr., for a copy of the 'Model of Charity' – an intriguing quirk of history.

3 William Fiennes, Lord Saye and Sele, to John Cotton, July 1638, in Sargent Bush, Jr. ed., *The Correspondence of John Cotton* (Chapel Hill: University of North Carolina Press, 2001) 283.

4   John Milton, 'Of Reformation', in Frank Allen Patterson ed., *The Works of John Milton*, Vol. III (New York: Columbia University Press, 1931) 5.

5   Peter Bulkeley, *The Gospel Covenant, or The Covenant of Grace Opened* (London: Printed by Matthew Simmons, 1651) 16, 431. An early, shorter edition appeared in 1646.

6   J. Franklin Jameson ed., *Johnson's Wonder-Working Providence, 1628-1651* (New York: Charles Scribner's Sons, 1910) 29.

7   Cotton Mather, *Magnalia Christi Americana, or The Ecclesiastical History of New-England* (Hartford: Silas Andrus and Son, 1852; reprint, Edinburgh: Banner of Truth, 1979) 118–22.

8   My understanding of Edwards is indebted primarily to the work of three historians, though none of them would necessarily agree in detail with my interpretation: George M. Marsden, *Jonathan Edwards: A Life* (New Haven: Yale University Press, 2003); Harry S. Stout, 'The Puritans and Edwards', in Nathan O. Hatch and Harry S. Stout (eds), *Jonathan Edwards and the American Experience* (New York: Oxford University Press, 1988); and Gerald R. McDermott, *One Holy and Happy Society: The Public Theology of Jonathan Edwards* (University Park: Pennsylvania State University Press, 1992).

9   Most of these sermons are available in M. X. Lesser ed., *Jonathan Edwards: Sermons and Discourses, 1734-1738*, Volume 19 in Harry S. Stout ed., *The Works of Jonathan Edwards* (New Haven: Yale University Press, 2001). Also, the *Works of Jonathan Edwards Online* (http://edwards.yale.edu/archive) is an indispensable resource. Sermons that touch significantly on the city on a hill include number 358 on Ephesians 5.25–7 (May 1735); 403 on Matthew 5.14 (July 1736); 423 on 2 Chronicles 23.16 (Fast Day, March 1737); 424 on Ezekiel 20.21–2 (Fast Day, March 1737); 430 on 2 Samuel 20.19 (May 1737); and 468 on Jeremiah 2.5 (Fast Day, April 1738).

10   Stout, 'The Puritans and Edwards', 144.

11   *Works of Jonathan Edwards*, 19: 540.

12   *Works of Jonathan Edwards*, 19: 541–4.

13   From a fast-day sermon on 2 Chronicles 23.16 preached in March 1737. Available in the *Works of Jonathan Edwards Online* (http://edwards.yale.edu/archive).

14   *Works of Jonathan Edwards*, 19: 548–9.

15   *Works of Jonathan Edwards*, 19: 654.

16   Sermon number 423 on 2 Chronicles 23.16. Available in the *Works of Jonathan Edwards Online* at http://edwards.yale.edu/archive.

17   *Works of Jonathan Edwards*, 19: 673–4.

18   *Works of Jonathan Edwards*, 19:759.

19   *Works of Jonathan Edwards*, 19:759.

20   *Works of Jonathan Edwards*, 19:763–7.

21 Ernest Lee Tuveson, *Redeemer Nation: The Idea of America's Millennial Role* (Chicago: The University of Chicago Press, 1968) 27–9; Sacvan Bercovitch, *The American Jeremiad* (Madison: The University of Wisconsin Press, 1978) 98–107; Stout, 'The Puritans and Edwards', 157; and McDermott, *One Holy and Happy Society*, 20–5 and *passim*.

22 'Rulers, by the very design of their institution, are ministers of God for good to the people; and their situation gives them a peculiar advantage to promote this benevolent design. They are placed on high, like a city set upon a hill: The people look up to them as their fathers, guides and guardians, and confide in their wisdom to devise the best means to alleviate their burdens, to promote their interests, and perpetuate their happiness. . . .' Samuel McClintock, 'Sermon on Occasion of the Commencement of the New-Hampshire Constitution', in Ellis Sandoz ed., *Political Sermons of the American Founding Era, 1730–1805*, Vol. 1, 2nd edn. (Indianapolis: Liberty Fund, 1998) 806.

23 John Adams, *Papers of John Adams*, Gregg L. Lint, et al. (eds), Volume 9: March 1780–July 1780 (Cambridge: Belknap Press of Harvard University Press, 1996) 62. Capitalization and punctuation modernized.

24 Alexis de Tocqueville, *Democracy in America and Two Essays on America*, translated by Gerald E. Bevan with an Introduction and Notes by Isaac Kramnick (London: Penguin, 2003) 36–56.

25 Frederick Douglass, *A Lecture on Our National Capital* (Washington, DC: Smithsonian Institution Press, 1978) 21. A digitized copy of Douglass's manuscript is available at the Library of Congress website.

Chapter Four

1 Reconstructing the story of how the Model of Christian Charity came to be published was possible only with the generous assistance of the archivists of the Massachusetts Historical Society and the New-York Historical Society. The institutional archives of both societies proved indispensable. Unfortunately, the documents most directly related to the preparation of the Model for publication have not survived.

2 'List of 22 Historical Books dated 1607–1728 – sent by F. B. Winthrop to the Reverend Samuel Miller, 30 January 1809', New-York Historical Society – Letters, 1804–1809.

3 *Collections of the Massachusetts Historical Society, For the Year 1792.* Volume 1 (Boston: Belknap & Hall, 1792) 1–2.

4 The standard history is Louis Leonard Tucker, *The Massachusetts Historical Society: A Bicentennial History, 1791–1991* (Boston: Massachusetts Historical Society, 1996).

5 George Folsom to Thaddeus M. Harris, 31 January 1838, Massachusetts Historical Society Archives, Massachusetts Historical Society.

6 Thaddeus M. Harris to George Folsom, 11 April 1838, George Folsom Papers, New-York Historical Society.

7   Joseph B. Felt to George Folsom, 18 April 1838, George Folsom Papers, New-York
    Historical Society.

8   'A Modell of Christian Charity', *Collections of the Massachusetts Historical Society*, 3rd
    series, Vol. VII (Boston: Little and Brown, 1838) 29–48.

9   *Collections of the Massachusetts Historical Society*, 3rd series, Vol. VII, 32.

10 *Collections of the Massachusetts Historical Society*, 3rd series, Vol. VII, 30.

11 All quotations from 'Address to the Young Men's Lyceum of Springfield, Illinois' in
    Abraham Lincoln: Speeches and Writings, 1832–1858 (New York: Library of America,
    1989) 28–36.

12 Lincoln's references to the 'rock' and the 'gates of hell' come from Matthew 16.18. The
    full verse reads, 'And I say also unto thee, That thou art Peter, and upon this rock I
    will build my church; and the gates of hell shall not prevail against it' (King James
    Version).

13 Harlow S. Sheidley, *Sectional Nationalism: Massachusetts Conservative Leaders and the
    Transformation of America, 1815–1836* (Boston: Northeastern University press, 1998)
    31, 118–47. See also Anne Norton, *Alternative Americas: A Reading of Antebellum
    Political Culture* (Chicago: The University of Chicago Press, 1986) 24–8, 257.

14 Peleg Sprague, 'An Address Delivered Before the Pilgrim Society of Plymouth,
    December 22, 1835' (Boston: Light and Stearns, 1836).

15 'The New England Character', *Southern Literary Messenger*, Vol. III, No. 6 (July 1837)
    413.

16 Unsigned review of *A History of the United States, From the Discovery of the American
    Continent to the Present Time*, by George Bancroft, Vol. I (Boston: Charles Bowen;
    London: R. J. Kennett [1834]) in *The Southern Literary Messenger*, Vol. I, No. 10
    (June 1835) 587–91. Quotations from 587–8 and 591. John Quincy Adams had used
    the phrase 'march of mind' to describe the American achievement in a July Fourth
    oration in 1821.

17 The standard biographies of Bancroft are Russel B. Nye, *George Bancroft: Brahmin
    Rebel* (New York: Alfred A. Knopf, 1945) and Lilian Handlin, *George Bancroft: The
    Intellectual as Democrat* (New York: Harper & Row, 1984). Three major collections
    of his extensive correspondence, papers and books are housed at the Massachusetts
    Historical Society, the New York Public Library, and Cornell University.

18 The publication history of Bancroft's *History of the United States* is extraordinarily
    complicated. The sixteenth edition (1858) includes the new material from the
    Model on pages numbered 357 and 357*. This odd pagination continued for several
    editions.

19 Bancroft, *History of the United States* (1834 edition) Vol. I: 377. Bancroft left these
    words virtually unchanged through the final edition in 1883.

20 Orestes Brownson, Review of George Bancroft, *History of the United States, From
    the Discovery of the American Continent*, Vol. IV (Boston: Little, Brown, 1852), in
    Brownson's Quarterly Review, Vol. VII, No. 4 (October 1852) 421, 423.

21 M. A. DeWolfe Howe, *The Life and Letters of George Bancroft*, Vol. I (New York: Charles Scribner's Sons, 1908) 226.

22 Michael Kraus, *The Writing of American History* (Norman: University of Oklahoma Press, 1953) 129.

23 John Gorham Palfrey, *History of New England*, Vol. I (Boston: Little, Brown: 1858) 312–13.

24 John Wingate Thornton, *The Pulpit of the American Revolution, or, The Political Sermons of the Period of 1776* (Boston: Gould and Lincoln, 1860).

25 First printed in December 1860 as a pamphlet under the title 'National Sins: A Fast-Day Sermon' and then reprinted in *The Southern Presbyterian Review*, Vol. XIII, No. 4 (January 1861) and in John B. Adger and John L. Girardeau (eds), Volume 4 of *The Collected Writings of James Henley Thornwell* (Richmond: Presbyterian Committee on Publication, 1873) 510–48.

26 James Henley Thornwell to George Bancroft, 26 January 1856, George Bancroft Papers, Massachusetts Historical Society.

27 *Our Triumph* (Richmond, VA: Soldiers' Tract Association, [1864]) 1.

28 S. A. Hodgman, *The Great Republic Judged, But Not Destroyed*, 2nd edn. (New York: Robert Craighead, 1865) 271–2.

29 *Report of the Commission to Procure Memorial Statues for the National Statuary Hall at Washington* (Boston: Albert J. Wright, 1877) 3–10.

30 Robert C. Winthrop, *Life and Letters of John Winthrop*, 1630–1649 (Boston: Ticknor and Fields, 1867). The excerpt is on pp. 18–20.

31 In 1888 the Model was excerpted in *A Library of American Literature*. Volume I (of 11) of that compendium included generous selections from Winthrop's journal and family letters and parts of the beginning and end of the Model, probably the longest excerpts reprinted since 1840 and possibly the discourse's first appearance in any literature anthology.

32 Moses Coit Tyler, *A History of American Literature, 1607–1765* (New York: C. P. Putnam's Sons, 1878). This classic textbook was reprinted in 1949 by Cornell University Press.

33 John Fiske, *The Beginnings of New England or The Puritan Theocracy in Its Relations to Civil and Religious Liberty* (London: Macmillan, 1889) 102.

34 G. E. Ellis, *The Puritan Age and Rule in the Colony of the Massachusetts Bay, 1629–1685* (Boston: Houghton, Mifflin, 1888) 56–7.

35 J. A. Doyle, *English Colonies In America*, Vol. II: *The Puritan Colonies* (New York: Henry Holt, 1889) 100–1.

36 Joseph Hopkins Twichell, *John Winthrop: First Governor of the Massachusetts Colony* (New York: Dodd, Mead, 1891) 60.

37 Herbert L. Osgood, *The American Colonies in the Seventeenth Century*, Vol. I: *The Chartered Colonies. Beginnings of Self-Government* (New York: Macmillan, 1904) 152–3, 205, 210.

38 Vernon L. Parrington, *Main Currents in American Thought: An Interpretation of American Literature From the Beginnings to 1920* (New York: Harcourt, Brace, 1927) I: iii, 27–50. The Foreword to this three-volumes-in-one edition is dated 1 January 1926. He drew his sources, including the Model of Christian Charity, almost exclusively from Robert C. Winthrop's *Life and Letters* with occasional citations of the journal.

39 Parrington, *Main Currents in American Thought*, 43.

40 *North American Review*, Vol. 104 (January 1867) 175.

Chapter Five

1 Samuel Eliot Morison ed., *The Humble Request of the Massachusetts Puritans, and A Modell of Christian Charity, by John Winthrop, 1630* (Boston: The Old South Association, 1917). The series of 'Old South Leaflets' began in the 1880s.

2 Samuel Eliot Morison, *Builders of the Bay Colony* (New York: Boston: Houghton Mifflin, 1930).

3 From the closing passages of *This Side of Paradise* (1920).

4 Morison, *Builders of the Bay Colony*, v, vi.

5 Morison, *Builders of the Bay Colony*, 72–4.

6 Stanley Gray, 'The Political Thought of John Winthrop', *The New England Quarterly*, Vol. 3, No. 4 (October 1930) 681–705, and Edgar A. J. Johnson, 'Economic Ideas of John Winthrop', *The New England Quarterly*, Vol. 3, No. 2 (April 1930) 235–50.

7 Reinhold Niebuhr, 'Perry Miller and Our Embarrassment', *The Harvard Review*, Vol. 2, No. 12 (1964) 49–51.

8 Perry Miller, 'The Influence of Reinhold Niebuhr', *The Reporter* (May 1, 1958) 39–40.

9 Morton White, 'Religion, Politics and the Higher Learning', *Confluence*, Vol. 3, No. 4 (December 1954) 404.

10 Perry Miller, *Errand into the Wilderness* (Cambridge: Harvard University Press, 1956) vii–viii.

11 Kenneth S. Lynn, 'Perry Miller', *The American Scholar* (Spring 1983) 221–7. For further biographical details, see also Robert Middlekauff, 'Perry Miller', in Marcus Cunliffe and Robin W. Winks (eds), *Pastmasters: Some Essays on American Historians* (New York: Harper & Row, 1969) 167–90, and Andrew Delbanco's entry on Miller in volume 15 of *American National Biography*.

12 Miller, *Errand into the Wilderness*, viii.

13 Perry Miller and Thomas H. Johnson, *The Puritans* (New York: American Book Company, 1938) vii, 181.

14 Perry Miller, *The New England Mind: The Seventeenth Century*, with a new preface by the author (Boston: Beacon Press, 1961) 418–19. This book was first published in 1939 and then reissued in 1954.

15 Miller, *Errand into the Wilderness*, 158.

16 Miller, *Errand into the Wilderness*, 11.

17 Miller, *Errand into the Wilderness*, 11–12.

18 Perry Miller, *The New England Mind: From Colony to Province* (Boston: Beacon Press, 1961) 5. This book was first published in 1953. See also p. 25 where Miller once more emphasized the transformative intention of the New England 'model'. This was why Winthrop chose the word 'model' for the title of his discourse, Miller argued, missing the point that Winthrop sketched a biblical model *within* the discourse for the Puritan colonists themselves to imitate.

19 Perry Miller, *Nature's Nation* (Cambridge: Belknap Press/Harvard University Press, 1967).

20 Miller, *Nature's Nation*, 6–8, 379–80.

21 Daniel J. Boorstin, *The Americans: The Colonial Experience* (New York: Vintage Books/Random House, 1958) 3–4.

22 Used by permission of Alfred Music Publishing.

23 Samuel Eliot Morison, *The Oxford History of the American People* (New York: Oxford University Press, 1965) 65, 1122.

24 Ted Sorensen, *Counselor: A Life at the Edge of History* (New York: Harper, 2008) 219–20.

25 *Life*, Vol. 48, No. 20 (23 May 1960).

26 *Life*, Vol. 49, No. 8 (22 August 1960). These essays were later collected into a volume edited by Harvard historian Oscar Handlin. After each essay in the book version (except Nixon's and Kennedy's) Handlin added a set of excerpts from relevant historical documents. The first document following the first essay was a section of the Model of Christian Charity, a document that had not been part of *Life*'s extensive national canon in 1960. But by the time the book appeared, Kennedy had used Winthrop's Model in his January 1961 farewell speech. Oscar Handlin ed., *American Principles and Issues: The National Purpose* (New York: Holt, Rinehart & Winston, 1961).

27 Kennedy's note cards for this address are available online through the Kennedy Library's digital archives (www.jfklibrary.org).

28 Richard S. Dunn, *Puritans and Yankees: The Winthrop Dynasty of New England, 1630–1717* (New York: W. W. Norton, 1962) 10–11.

29 Richard Schlatter, 'The Puritan Strain', in John Higham ed., *The Reconstruction of American History* (New York: Harper Torchbooks, 1962) 42.

30 Reinhold Niebuhr and Alan Heimert, *A Nation So Conceived: Reflections on the History of America from Its Early Visions to Its Present Power* (New York: Charles Scribner's Sons, 1963) 125.

31 Miller's military metaphors also left their mark on historian Loren Baritz's interpretation of the Puritan mission. See his *City on a Hill: A History of Ideas and Myths in America* (New York: John Wiley & Sons, 1964) 8, 14–18. For Darrett Rutman, the 'one phrase' about the city on a hill 'summed up [Winthrop's] thought' and 'reflected the core of his thinking'. Once again, these are claims it took Americans more than 300 years to arrive at. See Darrett Rutman, *Winthrop's Boston* (Chapel Hill: University of North Carolina Press, 1965) 3–4.

32 Ernest Lee Tuveson, *Redeemer Nation: The Idea of America's Millennial Role* (Chicago: University of Chicago Press, 1968).

33 Robert F. Kennedy, *RFK: Collected Speeches*, introduced by Edwin O. Guthman and C. Richard Allen (eds) (New York: Viking, 1993) 155–8.

Chapter Six

1 Godfrey Hodgson, *The Myth of American Exceptionalism* (New Haven, CT: Yale University Press, 2009) 1–3. Hodgson implicitly criticizes Reagan for calling Winthrop's ship the *Arabella* instead of the *Arbella* (without the extra 'a'), but the former spelling was common for centuries and used by other public figures, including John F. Kennedy.

2 John Patrick Diggins, *Ronald Reagan: Fate, Freedom, and the Making of History* (New York: W. W. Norton, 2007) 28, 30, 46, 165 and *passim*.

3 Hugh Heclo, 'Ronald Reagan and the American Public Philosophy,' in W. Elliot Brownlee and Hugh Davis Graham (eds), *The Reagan Presidency: Pragmatic Conservatism and Its Legacy* (Lawrence: University Press of Kansas, 2003) 18.

4 Ronald Reagan, *An American Life* (New York: Simon and Schuster, 1990) 299.

5 Ronald Reagan, *The Notes: Ronald Reagan's Private Collection of Stories and Wisdom*, Douglas Brinkley ed. (New York: Harper, 2011) 7.

6 Ronald Reagan, *Speaking My Mind: Selected Speeches* (New York: Simon and Schuster, 1989) 44.

7 Reagan, *Speaking My Mind*, 44.

8 All twelve of these speeches have been published in Ronald Reagan, *A City Upon a Hill: Speeches by Ronald Reagan Before the Conservative Political Action Conference, 1974–1988*, James C. Roberts (ed.) (Washington, D.C.: The American Conservative Union, 1989). Winthrop and/or the 'city upon a hill' appear in at least the first four of these speeches (25 January 1974; 1 March 1975; 6 February 1977; and 17 March 1978). In the 1978 speech, he added the word 'shining' to the city.

9 Reagan, *A City Upon a Hill*, 10, 20.

10 Ronald Reagan, *Reagan, In His Own Hand: The Writings of Ronald Reagan That Reveal His Revolutionary Vision for America*, with an introduction and commentary by Kiron K. Skinner, Annalise Anderson, and Martin Anderson (eds), with a foreword by George P. Schultz (New York: Free Press, 2001), xiv-xv, 13–14.

11 For examples of each of these quotations, see Ronald Reagan, *A Time for Choosing: The Speeches of Ronald Reagan, 1961–1982*, Alfred Balitzer ed. (Chicago: Regnery Gateway, 1983) 179, 201, 232, and 233.

12 Ronald Reagan, 'Official Announcement of Candidacy for President,' November 13, 1979, http://reagan2020.us/speeches/candidacy_announcement.asp. This online version capitalizes 'Pilgrim,' but Reagan did not, as his letter to John McClaughry makes clear. See Ronald Reagan, *Reagan: A Life in Letters*, Kiron K. Skinner, Annelise Anderson, and Martin Anderson (eds), with a foreword by George P. Schultz (New York: Free Press, 2003) 289–90.

13 Reagan, *Reagan: A Life in Letters*, 289–90.

14 The website of the Commission on Presidential Debates has a complete transcript of this debate. See http://www.debates.org/pages/trans80a_p.html.

15 Ronald Reagan, *Public Papers of the Presidents of the United States: Ronald Reagan, 1981: January 20 to December 31, 1981* (Washington, DC: Office of the Federal Register, National Archives and Records Service, General Services Administration, 1982) 938. Hereafter cited as *Public Papers* followed by year, book and page number.

16 *Public Papers*, 1983, Book 2: 1406–8.

17 *Public Papers*, 1984, Book 2: 1001.

18 *Public Papers*, 1986, Book 2: 1515.

19 *Public Papers*, 1988–1989, Book 2: 1078.

20 Richard Lingeman, 'Reagan Wins: The Hollow Man', *The Nation*, 15 November 1980, http://www.thenation.com/doc/19801115/lingeman.

21 Larry King, *Tell It to the King* (New York: G. P. Putnam's Sons, 1988) 99. See also William Safire, 'Rack Up That City On a Hill', *New York Times*, 24 April 1988.

22 Mario Cuomo, Democratic National Convention Keynote Address, 16 July 1984. A fairly accurate transcription of Cuomo's speech is available at http://www.americanrhetoric.com/speeches/mariocuomo1984dnc.htm. See also William Safire, 'Ringing Rhetoric', *New York Times*, 19 August 1984.

23 Videos of the complete speech are readily available on the Internet.

24 *Public Papers*, 1988–1989, Book 2: 1722.

25 *Public Papers*, 1988–1989, Book 2: 1736.

26 Ann Carey McFeatters, *Sandra Day O'Connor: Justice in the Balance* (Albuquerque: University of New Mexico Press, 2005) 193.

27 D. G. Hart, *From Billy Graham to Sarah Palin: Evangelicals and the Betrayal of American Conservatism* (Grand Rapids, MI: Eerdmans, 2011) 44–8.

28 Richard V. Pierard and Robert D. Linder, *Civil Religion and the Presidency* (Grand Rapids, MI: Academic Books/Zondervan, 1988) 257–8.

29 Pierard and Linder, *Civil Religion and the Presidency*, 274–80, 283.

30 Heclo, 'Ronald Reagan and the American Public Philosophy', 21–2, 35.

31 Roger Cohen, 'America Unmasked', *New York Times*, 26 April 2009, http://www.nytimes.com/2009/books/review/Cohen-t.html.

Chapter Seven

1 John Lukacs, *The Future of History* (New Haven: Yale University Press, 2011) 102.

2 Robert Middlekauff, *The Mathers: Three Generations of Puritan Intellectuals, 1596–1728* (New York: Oxford University Press, 1971) 26, 98–9.

3 John Winthrop to Margaret Winthrop, 15 May 1629, *Winthrop Papers*, Vol. II (Boston, Massachusetts Historical Society, 1931) 91–2.

4 Theodore Dwight Bozeman, 'The Puritans' "Errand into the Wilderness" Reconsidered', *The New England Quarterly*, Vol. 59, No. 2 (June 1986) 231; and Bozeman, *To Live Ancient Lives: The Primitive Dimension in Puritanism* (Chapel Hill: University of North Carolina Press, 1988) 120–2.

5 Andrew Delbanco, *The Puritan Ordeal* (Cambridge: Harvard University Press, 1989) 72. See also Delbanco, 'The Puritan Errand Re-Viewed', *Journal of American Studies*, Vol. 18, No. 3 (December 1984) 343–60.

6 Francis J. Bremer, *John Winthrop: America's Forgotten Founding Father* (New York: Oxford university press, 2003) 173–84. See also his earlier essay, 'To Live Exemplary Lives: Puritans and Puritan Communities as Lofty Lights', *The Seventeenth Century*, Vol. VII (1992) 27–39.

7 Kathleen Kenney Townsend, 'The Pursuit of Happiness: What the Founders Meant – And Didn't.' http://www.theatlantic.com/business/archive/2011/06/the-pursuit-of-happiness-what-the-founders-meant-and-didnt/240708/. Accessed 6/21/2011.

8 Robert Kagan, *Dangerous Nation* (New York: Alfred A. Knopf, 2006) 7–8 and notes.

9 David Gelernter, *Americanism: The Fourth Great Western Religion* (New York: Doubleday, 2007)1, 23, 66, 70, 208.

10 Sarah Palin, *Going Rogue: An American Life* (New York: Harper, 2009) 394.

11 Sarah Palin, *America By Heart: Reflections on Family, Faith, and Flag* (New York: Harper, 2010).

12 Palin, *America By Heart*, xvi.

13 Palin, *America By Heart*, 64.

14 Palin, *America By Heart*, 70.

15 Palin, *America By Heart*, 182, 205.

16 Text and video of Rubio's 14 June 2011 speech, 'The New American Century', is available at http://rubio.senate.gov.

17 Peter Marshall and David Manuel, *The Light and the Glory* (Grand Rapids, MI: Fleming H. Revell, 1977) 161–2, 168–9. A revised and expanded edition appeared in 2009.

18 R. A. Markus, *Saeculum: History and Society in the Theology of St. Augustine*, rev. ed. (Cambridge: Cambridge University Press, 1988) 44.

INDEX

An 'n.' after a page number indicates an endnote.